FOLLOWERSHIP IN THE TRI-STATES: VALUES AND BEHAVIORS DEEMED MOST DESIRABLE BY SMALL BUSINESS LEADERS

A Doctoral Dissertation Research

Submitted to the

Faculty of Argosy University,

Phoenix College of Business

In Partial Fulfillment of

The Requirements for the Degree of

Doctor of Business Administration

by

Dr. Thomas R. Steinback

July 2012

FOLLOWERSHIP IN THE TRI-STATES: VALUES AND BEHAVIORS

DEEMED MOST DESIRABLEBY SMALL BUSINESS LEADERS

Dissertation Committee Approval:

Anne F. Nelson, D.B.A.

Bob Goldwasser, D.B.A.

Bruce T. Strom, Ph.D.

Copyright © 2012

Dr. Thomas R. Steinback

ISBN: 1-4823-3793-2

ISBN13: 978-1482-3379-38

Dragon's Breath Publishing

ABSTRACT

Over the course of one's career lifetime, they will follow more than they will lead. There is an abundance of tips, guidelines, templates and traits on becoming a leader or manager, but what happens when a leader turns around and there is no one following them? Ideal followers are strategic to the success of the enterprise and the effectiveness of the leader, especially in small business where resources are limited and roles diverse. The 2007 Deckert study in North Florida examined LMX theory in the context of small business and provided an inspiration for this study.

Tri-States is a rural region in decline, struggling with an evolving global economy, brain drain, and the disappearance of Stage 4 businesses that employ 500 or more people. The region is heavily dependent on small business that created 93 percent of new jobs in the Tri-States from 1992-2008. In 2011 only eight of 15,639 total businesses represented were Stage 4 companies. Some of the key words and terms explored include: complexity economics, economic development, entrepreneurship, followership, high quality dyadic relationship (HQDR), instrumental values, leader, leader-member exchange (LMX) theory, leadership, manager, Rokeach value survey (RVS), Stage 2 & 3 companies, stages of entrepreneurship, stakeholder, and terminal values.

This quantitative research study demonstrates the role of value congruence between leaders and followers in achieving a high quality dyadic relationship. It also provides a baseline for small business owners in their quest for organizational excellence and emphasizes the value added benefit of viewing employees as strategic partners. This study further defines clear expectations small business leaders have for ideal followers and effective leadership.

ACKNOWLEDGEMENTS

The author expresses sincere gratitude to committee chair Dr. Anne Nelson, committee member Dr. Bob Goldwasser, Dr. Timothy Drake, and program chair Dr. Bruce T. Strom, for their unlimited support and guidance in the planning and implementation of this research project. Their encouragement, professionalism, and motivation were inspirational and vital to this journey over the past two years.

Dr. Nelson's constant encouragement and understanding as this researcher sometimes lost focus and wondered, was amazing! Thanks to the AUO IRB, this author narrowed his focus and fine-tuned the research project. Deepest appreciation is further offered to the small business managers and entrepreneurs across the Dubuque Tri-State area for their participation in this research study. The smaller the enterprise, the more passionate their resolve to help. Without their sincere interest and vital contribution of time and resources, this study would not have been possible.

Thanks go to Dr. Driver and the Panther Editing team for their assistance with research methodology and final proposal. Special thanks to Dr. Jim Baxter and his team from phd@statassist.com. Their patience, statistics work and APA editing with the final package, helped give polish and meaning to this researcher's effort and struggle. Dr. Baxter's belief in this author as a person first, will always be treasured. And last but not least: A.J., Clayton, Colter, Mark, Jakob, and Josh – thank you gentlemen for believing in me as your mentor and for wanting to be a part of my project -- your friendship and hard work inspires me.

DEDICATION

This doctoral journey began in August 2007 with the final dissertation phase commencing in September 2009. Fourteen months into the process the original research effort hit a snag and fell apart, forcing a readjustment and renewed effort that became this research project. While this author's path has been long and the journey tedious, this moment of closure would not have been possible without the relentless encouragement and moral support provided by a strong network of close personal friends. From beginning to end, Art, Bethany, Catharina, Jennifer, and Susan, while they may not have understood what the topic is all about, respected this writer for his passion and dream.

Thank you, all of you, from the bottom of my heart. Another dear friend deserving recognition here is Trudy, a cohort of mine from the start. Our parallel journey became a game of cat and mouse taking turns helping each other meet obstacles head on with creative solutions and encouragement. Thank you T, we did it!

And last but not least, a personal note for my daughters, Lindsay, Laurie, Chelsea and grandchildren, Isabelle, Breckin and Kiptyn. I hope you can someday appreciate why I dedicated this quest to Edward Senior, your grandfather and great grandfather. His life, from U.S. Army radio man to aerospace engineer blasting original astronauts into history, all without a formal college degree, inspired me since the age of twenty to accomplish this milestone. While my journey has been long, the lesson is to never give up on your dreams. You can be whatever you want to be, at any age.

Dad – this is for YOU!

TABLE OF CONTENTS

Page

TABLE OF TABLES   x

TABLE OF APPENDICES   xii

CHAPTER ONE: INTRODUCTION   1

The Problem   2

Problem Background   3

Purpose of the Study   6

Research Questions and Hypotheses   7

Significance of the Study   9

Limitations and Delimitations.   10

Definition of Terms.   10

Importance of the Study   13

Organization of the Remainder of the Tri-States Study.   13

CHAPTER TWO: LITERATURE REVIEW   14

Holistic Overview   14

Complexity Economics   16

Entrepreneurship and Innovation   17

Leadership.   21

Followership .   22

Leader-Member Exchange (LMX) Theory   25

Value-Behavior Relationship.   28

Defining Values   29

Value-Behavior Dynamic   30

LMX and Values   31

Small Business Challenges   32

Values Small Business Leaders Designate as Necessary to Succeed   36

Summary   39

CHAPTER THREE: METHODOLOGY   41

Research Design.   41

Research Questions and Hypotheses   43

Selection of Participants   46

Instrumentation   47

Sampling Protocol.   50

Data Processing and Analysis   51

Assumptions   53

Limitations   53

Delimitations.   54

Summary   54

CHAPTER FOUR: DATA ANALYSIS AND RESULTS   55

Introduction   55

Research Questions and Hypotheses   55

Data Collection .   58

Demographics   58

Data Analysis   59

     Research Question 1 Findings   59

     Research Question 2 Findings   60

     Research Question 3 Findings   62

     Research Question 4 Findings   63

     Research Question 5 Findings   64

     Research Question 6 Findings   66

     Research Question 7 Findings   67

Observations and Analysis of Survey Data   67

CHAPTER FIVE: DISCUSSIONS, CONCLUSIONS & RECOMMENDATIONS   73

Discussion of Findings.   73

Chapter One Synopsis.   73

Chapter Two Synopsis   73

Chapter Three Synopsis   75

Chapter Four Synopsis   76

Conclusions   77

Logistic Comparisons - North Florida versus Tri-States   77

Findings – North Florida versus Tri-States.   79

Implications for Practice   82

Recommendations for Further Research   83

REFERENCES   85

TABLE OF TABLES

Table   Page

2.1. Meilinger's (1994) Activities Defining Good Followership   23

2.2. Solovy's (2005) Activities Defining Good Followership   24

2.3. Kelley's 15 Attributes for Exemplary Followership   25

2.4. Summary of Small Businesses Contributions   34

2.5. Internal Factors for Small Businesses to Overcome   36

2.6. External Factors for Small Businesses to Overcome   37

3.1. RVS Values, Traits and Behaviors   46

4.1. Specified Design Components Related to the Seven Hypotheses   57

4.2. Top Three RVS Values For an Ideal Employee   60

4.3. Bottom Three RVS Values For an Ideal Employee   61

4.4. Top Three Most Important RVS Values Leaders
    Should Possess to Succeed   62

4.5. Top Three Least Important RVS Values Leaders
    Should Possess to Succeed   63

4.6. Generation by Top Three Most Important RVS Values
    For an Ideal Employee   65

4.7. Gender by Top Three Most Important RVS Values
    For an Ideal Employee   66

4.8. Top Three Ranked Industries by Top Three Most Important
    RVS Values For an Ideal Employee   68

4.9. Model Summary Generated from Multiple Regression
    Analysis of Generational Differences   70

4.10. Model Summary Generated from Multiple Regression
    Analysis of Industrial Differences   72

5.1. RVS Rankings: North Florida vs. Tri-States   79

5.1. Top and Bottom Three Ranked Values   79

5.2. Education & Experience: North Florida vs. Tri-States
    Percentage Distribution   81

TABLE OF APPENDICES

Appendix	Page
A. The Leader-Member Exchange (LMX) Model.	104
B. Stage 2 Business Clusters Across Dubuque Tri-States Market	105
C. Tri-States LMX Survey 2012	106
D. Five Big Ideas Behind Complexity Economics	112
E. Entrepreneurship Competency Model .	113
F. RVS Permissions- Attribution-ShareAlike 3.0 Unported (CC BY-SA 3.0)	114
G. Demographic Data Frequency Tables	115

CHAPTER ONE: INTRODUCTION

A contemporary study of modern leadership theory will uncover an abundance of research grounded in the idea that the promotion of leadership technique leads to professional success (Kelley, 1988, 1992). However, the opportunity for leadership is rare and limited to the span of one's career, which means most people will work as followers and only a few will actually rise to the rank of leader (Johnson, 2003). Although formal management programs, researchers, and studies attempt to dissect leadership traits and templates, the science of followership is only beginning (Deckert, 2007).

The emerging phenomenon of the science of followership is characterized increasing numbers of studies on the value of followership (Rosenau, 2004; Stewart, 2003). One such effort is leader-member exchange theory [LMX] (Dansereau, Graen, & Haga, 1975; Graen & Cashman, 1975), in which theorists critiqued leader-follower interaction and suggested ways to achieve a high quality dyadic relationship [HQDR] (Erdogan, Kraimer, & Liden, 2004). Another legitimate area of study is the manner in which LMX unfolds in a large company setting versus a small company setting where interpersonal dynamics can be more distinctive and the potential effect of reducing employee turnover and improving organizational effectiveness are increasingly profound (Deckert, 2007). Appendix A (Griffin& Moorhead, 2010) illustrates a holistic model of LMX theory.

Deckert (2007) performed a quantitative LMX research study of private small businesses across North Florida with 559 or fewer employees. Page 75 lists the Rokeach Value Survey (RVS) instrumental traits Deckert administered (Rokeach 1973; Rokeach & Ball-Rokeach, 1989), establishing a baseline for future LMX research studies of small businesses. Although five levels of participant education and experience were benchmarked, Deckert did not provide comparisons to other geographic locations and age, gender, or industry datasets were not identified. Considering the study, Deckert (2007) noted, "It would be interesting to replicate this research using geographic location as a demographic in order to attempt to further understand how leaders in different regions of the U.S. may seek different values and behaviors from their followers" (p. 80).

The Tri-States quantitative research study drew inspiration from Deckert's (2007) analysis of small businesses across North Florida; however, this study represents a unique and explicit effort in a rural setting with a cultural legacy rich in entrepreneurship, across three Tri-State counties: Dubuque (IA), Grant (WI), and Jo Daviess (IL). This effort will: (a) compare a rural location versus an urban one, (b) expand the sampling population targeted by Deckert (2007) by focusing on Stage 2 (10 to 99 employee) and Stage 3 (100 to 499 employee) companies as defined by the Edward Lowe Foundation (2011), and (c) benchmark gender, age and industry which were not specified in the original study. To maintain consistency, the same Rokeach Value Survey (RVS) instrument (Rokeach, 1973; Rokeach & Ball Rokeach, 1989) adapted by Deckert (2007) in North Florida was administered in the Tri-States study.

The Problem

For millennia, the phenomenon of leadership has been studied, recorded, and taught (Beckerleg, 2002). Historical records have been used to provide leadership stories from ancient Egypt 5,000 years ago (Paul, Costley, Howell, & Dorfman, 2002) and lessons by Xenophon, the Greek general, 2,000 years ago (Enzenauer, 2004). Chinese philosopher Lao-Tsu speculated about effective leadership traits in the 6th century (Owen, 2000). Following the historical pattern, recent leadership experts include contemporary researchers such as: Acs (1992), Bass (1985, 1990a, 1990b,), Bennis (1988, 1991, 1996, 2005), Drucker (1985, 2004), Gartner (1985a, 1985b, 1988, 1989), Graen, Dansereau, Minami, and Cashman (1973), Katz and Gartner (1988), Kotter (1997, 2000, 2006), and Zakaria (2009).

Collectively, researchers and theorists are evolving diverse views and theories of leadership, from the early 20th century's "Great Man" leadership traits (Northouse, 2004) to a variety of emerging leadership theories depicted by contingency leadership (Fiedler, 1964), situational leadership (Hersey & Blanchard, 1969), leader-member exchange (Dansereau et al., 1975), servant leadership (Greenleaf, 1977), transformational leadership (Burns, 1978, 2003), and Level-5 leadership (Collins, 2001). Popular leadership, organizational behavior, and entrepreneurship textbook authors (Griffin & Moorhead, 2010; Hackman & Johnson, 2009; Hisrich, Peters, & Shepherd, 2008) include all of these contemporary theories as the essence of leadership. The premise is that leadership is a valuable force to be studied and understood, regardless of whether such leadership is effective or ineffectual (Lundin & Lancaster, 1990).

While a study about leadership and why people lead may generate a variety of ideas, the question remains, what do we understand about the dynamics of why people follow? The simple reality is that fewer leaders than followers are produced. In addition, the number of leadership opportunities a person may experience in their lifetime is limited and may be rare (Johnson, 2003). "Followership dominates organizations; there are always more followers than leaders" (Dixon & Westbrook, 2003, p. 20).

Although leadership is taught in nearly every modern business management training program, the aspect of followership is rarely addressed (Hackman & Johnson, 2009; Kelley, 1988, 1992). One probable consequence is numerous missed opportunities for leaders of an organization to recognize, understand, and optimize the importance of the leader-follower exchange and how it can be leveraged to increase the organization's chances for success (Dixon & Westbrook, 2003). This reality has been viewed as undermining individuals and organizations alike (Kelley, 1988). Colangelo (2000) proposed that negative stereotypes distort the perceived meaning of followership. Kelley (1992) suggested negative images of a sheep mentality.

Leaders cannot lead without followers, yet logic indicates that followers can directly influence a leader's effectiveness and facilitate or derail goals of the leader and the organization alike: "It follows that the dynamics of leadership are intimately and inextricably tied up with followership" (Rosenau, 2004, p.16).

Although a growing number of contemporary researchers have recognized the value of effective followership, the absence of published material and curriculum activity advocating effective followership continues (Rusher, 2005). Lundin and Lancaster (1990) suggested, "thousands of pages have been written about leaders in organizations, very little has been written about followers" (p.19). This premise was reinforced by Wren (1995) who published The Leader's Companion, a compendium of leadership theory in which the phenomenon of leader-follower theory only accounted for 10% of the content in the text that was dominated by traditional leadership theory. As the discourse regarding leader-follower exchange continues, several emerging ideas may be used to sustain the effort to study and value effective followership. Sergiovanni (1990) advocated integrating the principles and practices of effective followership into the nation's Kindergarten through 12th-grade school system. Dixon and Westbrook (2003) recommended that company leaders incorporate visible reward programs and active followership training for employees at all levels in the organization.

Problem Background

The U.S. Department of Agriculture (Drabenstott & Moore, 2009) defines the Rural Midwest as an area consisting of 12 states: North Dakota, South Dakota, Nebraska, Kansas, Missouri, Iowa, Minnesota, Wisconsin, Illinois, Indiana, Michigan, and Ohio. The same region has been labeled by the U.S. Census Bureau as America's Heartland and the population center for the country (Drabenstott, 2008; Drabenstott & Moore, 2009). In the middle of the Heartland are 21 counties known as the Riverlands Region (see Appendix B), and at the epicenter of the Riverlands is the city of Dubuque, Iowa, where the Wisconsin and Illinois borders meet Iowa at the Mississippi River. Together, the three counties of Dubuque (IA), Grant (WI), and Jo Daviess (IL) form an area locally known as the Tri-States.

The Tri-State's historical legacy began with agriculture, education, engineering, and mining, and founded by pioneering leaders who were the region's earliest entrepreneurs (Drabenstott, 2008). Alexander Hamilton Willard and Nathaniel Hale Poor were original members of the Lewis and Clark expedition and had established business ties to Grant County (Rural Policy Research Institute, 2008). President Ulysses S. Grant owned a family leather business in Jo Daviess County; A. Y. McDonald was a pioneering steamfitter and plumbing inventor in Dubuque County; and John Deere emerged from the region as an innovative manufacturer of state-of-the-art farm implements (Rural Policy Research Institute, 2009).

Regardless if these individuals guided a family business, an expedition, or an army, they were leaders with followers and the success of their ventures was proportionate to the quality of people they led (Drabenstott, 2010).

The study of leader-member exchange from the perspective of the small business leader provides a benchmark of preferred values those leaders desire their followers to possess in order to achieve organizational success. This also enables the leaders of largest employer segment in the region to increase their chances at surviving and thriving (Gibbons, 2006, 2010) in the midst of difficult economic times.

Across the Tri-States, small business owners/entrepreneurs are among the first to recognize the immediate benefit of effective leadership and followership. If a small Stage 2 business leader diminishes leader-follower bonds, and five people quit out of a workforce of 9 or 10 minimum, half of the workforce has been lost in a labor market that is typically tight, understaffed, and subject to intense competition (Drabenstott, 2008; Drabenstott & Moore, 2009; Rural Policy Research Institute [RUPRI], 2008, 2009).

Regardless of the circumstance, the evolutionary process of business development over time has been driven by collaborative entrepreneurs in all facets of the community and any opportunity to improve organizational effectiveness should not be overlooked (Beinhocker, 2007).

The Wisconsin Way recently classified Wisconsin's current situation as a "train wreck, and not sustainable" (Wood, 2010, p. 1). The Wisconsin Competitiveness Study, also reinforced this idea by stating: "The rapid change that has defined the knowledge economy and the Internet era has punished those who have been slow to adapt and learn new skills," (Buelow & Hess, 2010, p. 4). Although unsettling, chaos and uncertainty are catalysts for innovation and entrepreneurship (Gibbons, 2010; Gibbons & Lange, 2010).

At the same time, as economic times become more difficult, the need for leaders to identify and sustain quality team members increases.

The train wreck Wood (2010) described is deeply troubling for small company leaders in the Tri-States region because the Heartland is home for 5 of the top 8 states in the USA for factory concentration, and 5 of the top 8 states in the U.S. for the number of farm proprietors (Atkinson & Andes, 2008; Drabenstott & Moore, 2009, p. 15-17). The current economic uncertainty can be used to create opportunity:

> The rural Midwest has a choice between two futures. It can continue to decline, or it can reinvent itself to compete in the global economy, as regions around the world are now doing. The first choice is not acceptable, but the second demands a new path to development and prosperity. (Drabenstott & Moore, 2009, p. 1)

One element of managerial reinvention is a better understanding of those values leaders deem most important for their followers to possess and signifies a new path in leadership. Gartner (1985b) characterized moments like this as watershed events. Arikan (2010) suggested local values and cultural factors are potential barriers to entrepreneurs.

In that context, Gibbons (2010) believed transformation would be dramatic and spark radical change throughout the social network. As a result, champions arise as change agents, new social networking bridges are created, and the potential for incremental growth is sustained as progressive levels of transformation are achieved (Kaufmann Foundation & International Economic Development Council [IEDC], 2008).

According to Lesa Mitchell, Executive Vice President of the Kaufmann Foundation (2009), after years of targeted sponsorship, Kaufmann concluded that traditional academia has not fully accomplished the Foundation's goal of making entrepreneurship a culture and destination, pursuing instead a path of extemporaneous activity that fosters minimal collaboration and limited cooperation. Effective collaboration and cooperation sits at the natural value of entrepreneurs who trust their peer Chief Executive Officer (CEO) colleagues more than they trust anyone else (Gibbons, 2006, 2010). As CEOs discover new ideas related to LMX theory they will be inclined to share that information with their peer networks (Deckert, 2007).

Across the Tri-States there are 15,639 total businesses and of that number, only eight employ 500 people or more (Edward Lowe Foundation, 2011). The remaining 15,139 are segmented into 65 Stage 3 businesses comprised of 100 to 499 employees, 1,214 Stage 2 businesses comprised of 10 to 99 employees, 8,063 Stage 1 businesses comprised of 2 to 9 employees, and 6,289 self-employed individuals, also known as sole proprietors (Edward Lowe Foundation, 2011; InfoUSA, 2011). Stage 2 and Stage 3 companies are significant because from 1992 through 2008 that segment across the Tri-States Market, specifically accounted for 51% of the total new jobs created. In contrast,

Stage 4 companies only accounted for 7% of the new jobs. This reality provides a primary motivation behind this study focusing on that segment (Edward Lowe Foundation, 2009; Gibbons, 2010; InfoUSA, 2011).

A study of leadership should begin with an overview of history (Sobel, 2006), progressing from the earliest days of hunter-gatherers who struggled to survive, to the advent of global manufacturers seeking to balance supply chains serving diverse markets. Although Maasi tribesmen measured wealth on the size of an individual's cattle herd and advanced technologists created wealth from a virtual domain, members of both cultures have been entrenched in the dynamics of leader-follower relationships. The innovative process of creative destruction entrepreneurs use to create wealth and inspire competition can be used in studies of leader-follower relationships to formulate templates for success (Gartner, 1985b; Sobel, 2006).

The phenomenon of entrepreneurial leadership has resulted in scholars building model templates of traits and/or behaviors that can be followed (Beckerleg, 2002). Social scientist, Gartner (1989), recommended that researchers seek to understand two basic ideas: first, differences between entrepreneurs (leaders) versus non-entrepreneurs (followers); and second, differences between entrepreneurs themselves.

Drucker (1985) pushed this rationale beyond lists of personality traits advocating instead, that entrepreneurs be examined in a context of practice and not personality. Leader practice is another way to examine behavior, and the concept is at the center of leader-follower relationships. Haslam and Platow (2001) introduced a more volatile sense of leader dynamics suggesting the "leader's capacity to engender active followership is contingent on their ability to promote collective interests with a shared in-group identity," (p. 1469).

Purpose of the Study

Dansereau, Graen, and Haga (1975) initially unveiled leader-member exchange (LMX) theory and provided seminal work exploring concepts of dyad linkages. Recently, leader-member exchange has been used interchangeably with leader-follower exchange and categorized by some as a descriptive leadership theory as opposed to a prescriptive one, with an emphasis on the process through which relationships form between leaders and followers (Northouse, 2004). This expanded on research by Haslam and Platow (2001) who suggested the dynamics of LMX exchange are very complex and fluid. Collinson (2006) questioned the conventional wisdom of tagging labels on leader identity and stated "identity pre-occupation can restrict their understanding of followers and ultimately constrain effective practice," (p. 187).

A thorough review of LMX theory is addressed in Chapter 2. Originally two main states for classifying leaders was outlined: the in-group (favored members), and the out-group (non-favored members). The dynamics of each group are unique and directly shape the nature of the leader–member relationship.

In the spirit of complexity economics and the process of evolutionary dynamics, LMX is an emerging and contemporary theory that is used by theorists to benchmarks various stages of relationship-building (Graen &Uhl-Bien, 1991, 1995). Proponents of LMX have emphasized the possibility that each participant in the LMX dyad can benefit when a high-quality relationship is achieved, also known as a high quality dyadic relationship (Dansereau et al., 1975; Graen & Cashman, 1975; Graen & Uhl-Bien, 1991, 1995; Spangenburg, 2004). The premise indicated a mutual benefit to each participant, and the dependency on each to understand what are the other's value expectations and behaviors (Fernandez & Hogan, 2002).

Rokeach (1973) described two values: instrumental and terminal. Instrumental values are linked to conduct and behavior, whereas terminal values pertain to the post relationship state. A high quality dyadic relationship shows a mutual understanding by both parties of the conduct and behavior desired by the other, the available range of options for instrumental values, and associated behaviors either party may choose to engage in or avoid (Fisher & Gitelson, 1983; Maierhofer, Griffin, & Sheehan, 2000; Schein, 1985). Although much information is available about the science of leadership and related traits, little is known about followership practices or processes (Lundin & Lancaster, 1990; Rusher, 2005). People who aspire to become effective leaders have numerous resources available (Kelley, 1988, 1992). While some emerging information is available on what followers expect from leaders, a gap exists between known expectations of followers and what leaders expect of followers (Lundin & Lancaster, 1990; Rusher, 2005).

Further studies of leader-follower behavior can bridge the divide. Human resource researchers have concentrated on large companies rather than small businesses (Chell & Tracey, 2005; Heneman, Tansy, & Camp, 2000; Hornsby & Kuratko, 1990, 2003). The need to expand the body of knowledge in the area of small business is reinforced by the significant effect small business owners have on local economies (Small Business Administration, 2006). As a result, information can be identified that improves small business performance and leader-follower effectiveness, and the information will be used in a positive manner for businesses and the community (Gartner & Bhat, 2000).

Heneman and Berkley (1999) suggested that a critical human resource challenge is in the ability of small business leaders to effectively staff and sustain quality employees. Philbrick, Dart, and Hass (1999) recommended the use of effective psychometric pre-employment screening instruments to enhance the staffing process, reduce turnover, improve morale, and optimize organizational performance. According to Deckert (2007) "a better understanding of the leader-follower dynamic will assist companies in developing more effective screening methods for filtering out individuals who may not have the follower values and associated behaviors that small business leaders deem most desirable for a follower to possess," (p. 6).

The Tri-States study will contribute to a combined body of knowledge by focusing specifically on the followership dynamic within small businesses. This information may empower individuals who perform in followership roles based on the knowledge of which values small business leaders deem most important or least important, by providing then with the ability to engage in or improve on those behaviors and associated behaviors identified as most important to developing a high quality dyadic relationship with the leader.

Research Questions and Hypotheses

The Tri-States study utilized an established quantitative survey questionnaire, the Rokeach Values Survey (Rokeach, 1973), to generate primary data for completing comparison research analysis (Simon & Francis, 2001). This study will utilize the same Rokeach Value Survey adapted for use by Deckert (2007) in North Florida and invite Tri-State leader participants to rank order a list of 18 instrumental values and associated behaviors as directed.

The original two primary research questions contained two variables each, framed as two-part questions. For clarity, each has been restated in this study as four separate research questions with a hypothesis (Ha) and null hypothesis (H0) for each question. Because the null hypothesis is known as the hypothesis of no difference, it will be clearly stated.

Participant responses are unique and subject to each person's preference based on their setting and culture. To be consistent with the Deckert (2007) study, the top three values ranked by each leader will be considered the most important and the lowest three values ranked will be considered the least important. In addition, variables of age, gender, and industry will be evaluated to understand any affect that may be imposed on results. Seven variables will be evaluated.

Research Question 1 (RQ1). When asked to describe an ideal follower using a list of instrumental values and associated behaviors outlined in the Rokeach Value Survey [RVS] (Deckert, 2007), which instrumental values and associated behaviors will small business leaders rank most important for followers to possess?

H1$_0$. There is no difference in most important RVS instrumental values and associated behaviors as they relate to those ideal followers should possess.

H1a . There is a difference in most important RVS instrumental values and associated behaviors as they relate to those ideal followers should possess.

Research Question 2 (RQ2). When asked to describe an ideal follower using a list of instrumental values and associated behaviors outlined in the Rokeach Value Survey [RVS] (Deckert, 2007), which instrumental values and associated behaviors will small business leaders rank least important for followers to possess?

H2$_0$. There is no difference in least important RVS instrumental values and associated behaviors as they relate to those ideal followers should possess.

H2a . There is a difference in least important RVS instrumental values and associated behaviors as they relate to those ideal followers should possess.

Research Question 3 (RQ3). What are the most important RVS values and associated behaviors small business leaders should possess to succeed as a leader?

H3$_0$. There is no difference in most important RVS values and associated behaviors a leader should possess in order to succeed as a leader.

H3a . There is a difference in most important RVS values and associated behaviors a leader should possess in order to succeed as a leader.

Research Question 4 (RQ4). What are the least important RVS values and associated behaviors small business leaders should possess to succeed as a leader?

H40 . There is no difference in least important RVS leader values and associated behaviors a leader should possess in order to succeed as a leader.

H4a . There is a difference in least important RVS leader values and associated behaviors a leader should possess in order to succeed as a leader.

Research Question 5 (RQ5). Does age positively affect RVS rankings?

H50 . There is no difference in RVS values as ranked by leaders due to age.

H5a . There is a difference in RVS values as ranked by leaders due to age.

Research Question (RQ6). Does gender positively affect RVS rankings?

H60 . There is no difference in RVS values as ranked by leaders due to gender.

H6a . There is a difference in RVS values as ranked by leaders due to gender.

Research Question 7 (RQ7). Does industry positively affect RVS rankings?

H70 .There is no difference in RVS values as ranked by leaders due to industry.

H7a . There is a difference in RVS values as ranked by leaders due to industry.

Significance of the Study

The problem is that small business managers have difficulty defining the attributes they want followers to possess in order to achieve high quality dyadic relationships. According to Ronsenau (2004), contemporary teaching models have embellished the role of leadership by making it seem absolute and larger than it should appear. In contrast, the role of followership is noteworthy and the nature of the LMX relationship is so complex that often it may not be clear at a given moment "who is leading and who is following" (Ronsenau, p.17).

Effective followership is strategic and can be used to motivate people to change their behavior roles and adopt successful leadership models that are used to recognize leader-follower needs. This is a challenge because negative stereotypes and perceptions persist across the business community and need to be overcome (Colangelo, 2000; Kelley, 1992).

This study examines two items of significance. First, is the theory that members can be empowered within the high quality dyadic relationship by helping each other understand the values and behaviors each member expects because of the relationship process prescribed in LMX theory (Dansereau et al., 1975).

For the process to be actualized and for the leader-follower relationship to reach optimal potential of becoming a positive relationship, each member should act in accordance with the other's expectations regarding the values and behaviors expected of each from the other (Deckert, 2007; Erdogan et al., 2004; Fernandez & Hogan, 2002; Maierhofer et al., 2000).

The second significant item is that the beneficiaries of final survey findings extend beyond individuals in the LMX relationship to the small business leaders who capitalize on outcomes by improving internal administrative procedures and implementing improved hiring profiles for future hires, which will improve employee morale, reduce negative costs of turnover, and enhance organizational effectiveness (Heneman & Berkley, 1999). A major goal in the Deckert (2007) study was to provide markers or suggestions that small business leaders could follow in improving their new hire screening and profiling activity by better matching an individual interest with LMX values specific to that unique small business enterprise. The same goals exist with the Tri-States study.

Limitations and Delimitations

Limitations include: (a) lingering uncertainty associated with the 2008/2009 recession and the perceived affect by owners on business operations; (b) the standardized RVSA instrument (Rokeach, 1973; Rokeach & Ball-Rokeach, 1989) as used in North Florida is shown in Appendix C. Demographics will be modified to collect data on age, gender, and industry, with customized cover letters and distribution protocols to reflect local requirements and Argosy University IRB requirements.

Delimitations include: (a) the target sample population is geographically confined to three Tri-State counties of Dubuque, Grant, and Jo Daviess; (b) the target population will only consist of Stage 2 (10 to 99 employees) and Stage 3 (100 to 499 employees) private for-profit companies; (c) only small business managers will be sampled in the survey for the leader's perspective; and (d) the correlation of age, gender, and industry data produced in the Tri-States research.

Definition of Terms

Complexity economics. Complexity economics (CE) is an emerging view of economics research embracing five "big ideas" that set it apart from traditional economics: dynamics, agents, networks, emergence, and evolution (Beinhocker, 2007, pp. 96-97). A fundamental premise of CE (see Appendix D) is that the economy is an evolutionary system and it goes beyond traditional economics, seeking the value of a tangible item, to a new dimension seeking to understand why choices are made.

Economic development. Economic development is described by the officials of the Economic Development Administration (EDA) as the foundation on which communities cultivate sustainable job growth and a viable regional economy by using two key economic drivers: innovation and regional collaboration (U.S. Department of Commerce, [EDA], 2010a, 2010b, & 2010c).

Entrepreneurial breadth and depth. Entrepreneurial breadth and depth is a measurement-based formula used by the Federal Reserve Bank in Kansas City to distinguish between rural-based entrepreneurial activity and urban-based entrepreneurial activity. In terms of total numbers, rural areas tend to have more entrepreneurs, many of whom are lifestyle entrepreneurs that enhance the quality of life, in contrast to urban areas that have a higher concentration of high-value entrepreneurs who create wealth (Low, Henderson & Weiler, 2005).

Entrepreneurs. Entrepreneurs are managers who function as change agents and decision makers (Edward Lowe Foundation, 2010a). "As owners, entrepreneurs are risk bearers. They reap the rewards for innovative, entrepreneurial success and bear the consequences of failure" (Low et al., 2005, p. 63). Appendix E shows an overview of an entrepreneurship competency model portraying a variety of tasks or competencies associated with entrepreneurs (Ennis, 2008).

Entrepreneurship. Entrepreneurship is defined as "the process of discovering new ways of combining resources" (Sobel, 2006, p. 1).

Follower. A follower is a person working under the "formal or informal supervision, oversight, direction, or leadership of another who has operational responsibility over the follower's daily activities, duties, and tasks" (Yukl, 2002, p. 8).Followers respond to ideas, in contrast to subordinates, who respond to authority (Sergiovanni, 1990).

Followership. Followership is the practice or process of independently performing tasks, critical thinking, constructive two-way dialogue, spontaneous innovation and creativity, while fully participating in collaborative decision-making (Banutu-Gomez, 2004).

Innovation. Innovation is a process of introducing or doing something new; the energy driving creative destruction or change creating new levels of performance (Drucker, 1985). Closely aligned with entrepreneurship (Flamholtz & Randle, 2007), innovation and entrepreneurship are integral to knowledge spillover (Acs, Braunerhjelm, Audretsch, & Carlsson, 2009).

Instrumental values. Instrumental values are values that are used to portray conduct or behavior that is "personally or socially preferable to an opposite or converse mode of conduct" (Rokeach, 1973, p. 5).

Leader (general definition). As a general definition, a leader is an individual who intentionally demonstrates influence "over other people to guide, structure, and facilitate activities and relationships in a group or organizations" (Yukl, 2002, p. 8).

Leader (research participant). A leader, in the context of a participant in LMX-based research efforts, holds the title of manager or supervisor in the target company (Kunze, 2006; Minsky, 2002).

Leader-member exchange (LMX) theory. LMX is role-making and relationship development between leaders and their followers (Dansereau et al., 1975; Graen & Cashman, 1975) with the goal of showing how leaders "will treat individual followers differently based on the quality of the individual relationship that exists between the leader and a follower" (Deckert, 2007, p. 12).

Leadership. Leadership is a diverse process of exercising operational control and setting policy (Katz & Kahn, 1978), establishing vision and goals (Rauch & Behling, 1984), building team unity and commitment (Drath & Palus, 1994), "fostering cultural values which create supportive environments that sustain the organization" (Richards & Engle, 1986, p. 206). Ultimately, a leader is one who can effectively "influence, motivate, and enable others to contribute towards the effectiveness and success of the organization" (House, Spangler, & Woycke, 1991, p. 184).

Manager. A manager is defined as a problem-solver who achieves optimal results that ensure people add value to the enterprise (Zaleznik, 1992). Metropolitan county. A Metropolitan county is a county with at least one city with a population of 50,000 people or more, such as Dubuque County (Drabenstott & Moore, 2010; Low et al., 2005).

Micropolitan county. A Micropolitan County is defined as a county with at least one city with a population of 10,000 to 50,000 people, such as Jo Daviess County (Drabenstott & Moore, 2010; Low et al., 2005).

Organization. An organization is "collectivities oriented to the pursuit of relatively specific goals and exhibiting relatively highly formalized social structures" (Scott, 2003. p. 27).

Rokeach Value Survey (RVS). A list of 18 words that survey participants rank order based on those they perceive as most important to those they deem as least important. Each participant's response is unique and the application of the same list to leaders or followers provides for uniform consistency, depending on the intended research focus. The 18 values with associated behaviors are listed in Table 7 (Deckert 2007; Rokeach & Ball-Rokeach, 1989).

Stage 2 companies. Stage 2 companies are considered growth-oriented entrepreneurships that employ 10-99 people. Leaders of Stage 2 companies create wealth and sustain long-term economic development, and embrace and launch radical innovation (Drabenstott &Moore, 2010; Edward Lowe Foundation, 2009, 2010a, 2010b, 2011; Gibbons, 2006; Gibbons & Lange, 2010; Quello, 2010).

Stages of entrepreneurship. Stages of entrepreneurship are defined by the officials of the Edward Lowe Foundation (2009, 2010a, 2010b, 2011) as follows: Self- Employed (sole proprietor), Stage 1 (2 to 9 employees), Stage 2 (10 to 99 employees), Stage 3 (100 to 499 employees), and Stage 4 (500+ employees). Each signifies a natural evolutionary step in the business cycle, from business creation to becoming the largest of publicly held enterprises, through which the owners experience an increasing span of control that distances the founder from the heart of the business, making them more dependent on intermediaries to function (Flamholtz & Randle, 2007).

Stakeholder. Nuseibeh and Easterbrook (2000) defined stakeholders as "individuals and organizations who stand to gain or lose from the success or failure of a system," (p.3). While the role of diverse stakeholders may be in conflict and intense, Boutelle (2004) established that the divergent views and interests stakeholders represent are vital in forming effective operational plans.

Town county. A town county is a county with no cities larger than 10,000 people, such as Grant County (Drabenstott & Moore, 2010; Low et al., 2005).

Importance of the Study

Tri-States responded to Deckert's (2007) call for further research, increasing as a result, the body of knowledge by accepting a core tenet of the North Florida study: LMX theory is a strategic tool used to identify preferred values leaders expect followers to model, and provide followers a blueprint of values and behaviors most likely to succeed in their leader's eyes, by achieving a high quality dyadic relationship with their leader (Deckert, 2007). Tri-States targeted a sampling population of small business leaders across the Tri-States region using probability-based simple random sampling methods (Cooper & Schindler, 2003, 2008), reinforced by direct solicitation of the target population to optimize response rates.

One goal for the Tri-States study was to provide a baseline for making a comparison of findings specific to the Tri-States geographic market in contrast to findings from the North Florida study. As a result, the body of LMX knowledge is expanded by providing a needed geographic comparison called for by Deckert (2007). At the same time, three new areas of understanding are achieved through evaluating the potential effect of age, gender, and industry on RVS rankings by the participating small business leaders. Although Deckert (2007) stated a goal was to identify opportunities for improving small business staffing and hiring activity, actual solutions and tools were not addressed. Similarly, those items were beyond the focus of theTri-States study.

Organization of the Remainder of the Tri-States Study

Chapter Two involves a literature review of the LMX theory and associated topics. Chapter Three describes research methodology to be used for the quantitative research study, Chapter Four reviews collected data with an analysis of findings, and Chapter Five summarizes the conclusions drawn based on the research study followed by recommendations for future research.

CHAPTER TWO: LITERATURE REVIEW

The Tri-States study utilized quantitative research methods applied by Deckert (2007) in his study of Central Contractor Registry (CCR) listed small businesses in North Florida, administering the Rokeach Value Survey (Rokeach, 1973; Rokeach & Ball- Rokeach, 1989) to leader managers in the targeted population. To be consistent with Deckert's research, this effort dwelled on the aspects of followership and the science of follower dynamics. Tri-States focuses on the leader and those behaviors he or she prefers to see in valued followers that contribute to the organization's success. This led to the premise that the easier it becomes for a leader to identify preferred follower behaviors and then benchmark future hiring with those standards, the more effective and successful the total follower group it becomes in helping the enterprise succeed.

While the Tri-States study is focused on the leader, the literature review is organized to provide the reader with a holistic overview of leadership and related challenges posed by researchers as it relates to the study. A series of relevant theory is presented: complexity economics, entrepreneurship and innovation, leadership, followership, leader-member exchange theory (LMX), value-behavior relationship, defining values, value-behavior dynamic, LMX and values, Stage 2 business challenges, and values that Stage 2 and Stage 3 business leaders deem as necessary to succeed.

Holistic Overview

A holistic overview of leadership and associated topics has identified an abundance of research articles and studies whereas a comparable list of information related to followership shows significantly fewer studies (Hollander, 1985; Lundin & Lancaster, 1990). The disparity between the number of leadership studies and the number of followership studies was in synchronization with the reality that the number of leadership opportunities a person may experience in a lifetime will be less than the number of followership roles experienced in a lifetime (Hollander, 1995). Followers outnumber the smaller population of leaders in the workforce at large (Johnson, 2003).

The disparity between leaders and followers is amplified by emerging recognition that early leadership research was framed by a perception that leadership was the single biggest predictor for a company's likelihood of success, while followership was perceived as having little or no significance (Banatu-Gomez, 2004). "Research on leadership has historically been heavily leader-focused with little attention paid to followers," (Collinson, 2006, p. 179).

In the context of early leadership research, a basic question was not asked: What happens when followers are not effective or do not follow? Subsequent contemporary researchers have identified essential competencies associated with effective followership including critical thinking, independence, innovation and creativity, and the ability to give and receive constructive criticism (Colangelo, 2000; Kelley, 1988, 1992). Collinson (2006) offered a list of adjectives used by contemporary researchers to describe effective followers such as, courageous, exemplary, and star, suggesting such desirable behaviors are precursors to organizational success and replace negative worker/follower stereotypes. Rusher (2005) suggested that researcher's slow recognition of positive followership traits reinforced negative stereotypes on followership. The subjectivity of early researchers and their discussion of transactional versus transformational leadership was outlined by Haslam and Platow (2001) as a key challenge and when measuring the effectiveness of a leader, it "hinges on their ability to turn 'me' into 'us' and to define a social project that gives that sense of 'us-ness' meaning and purpose," (p. 1471).

Yet, contemporary researchers are examining the science of followership and its strategic role in the leadership dynamic (Rosenau, 2004; Stewart, 2003). In the expanded view of followership, researchers have embraced a simple premise that if leaders have a better understanding of why people follow, their effectiveness as leaders and in teams will be enhanced (Bennis, 2005,2009; Rosenau 2004; Stewart 2003).

Leader-member exchange (LMX) theorists defined the relationship dynamic between leaders and followers (Dansereau et al., 1975; Graen & Cashman, 1975). The extent to which each member in the dynamic is engaged in values and behaviors mutually beneficial to the other is directly proportionate to the success of the exchange (Fernandez & Hogan, 2002). Knowledge used to facilitate the process effectively is essential to achieving a successful leader-follower exchange and reinforce the level of understanding small business leaders will achieve in the values and behaviors they want their employee-followers to emulate (Maierhofer, Griffin, & Sheehan, 2000; Schein, 1985).

Before examining the essential components of LMX theory, the topic of complexity economics [CE] (Beinhocker, 2007) will be examined. CE is a contemporary view of traditional economics that emerged after World War II (Beinhocker, 2007). CE theorists asked why people make the choices they do, especially when those choices are deliberately flawed, and the role of choice is vital to understanding why people both lead and follow (Beinhocker, 2007). Entrepreneurship and innovation are also examined.

Entrepreneurs envision, launch, and manage small businesses; therefore, it is important to examine the process entrepreneurs undertake and draw upon the work of scholars such as Drucker (1985), Gartner (1989), Sherwood (2002), and Sobel (2006). The process also includes the role of innovation because it is an essential driver in the entrepreneurial process. Research by Low et al. (2005), Loewe and Dominiquini (2006), and Drabenstott and Moore (2009) will be briefly examined, as well as the innovative role LMX researchers are pursuing to better understand the values and behaviors leaders of small companies prefer their followers to demonstrate.

A historical foundation of leadership and followership will be established by reviewing the literature presented by Bass (1985, 1990a), Bennis (1996), Burns (2003), Dixon and Westbrook (2003), Katz and Kahn (1978), Lundin and Lancaster (1990), Rosenau (2004), and Rusher, (2005). A critique of the literature involving LMX theory (Dansereau et al., 1975) will be reviewed. Research literature regarding value-behavior relationships will be examined in conjunction with seminal research by Rokeach (1973), and related research findings (Jehn, Chadwick, & Thatcher, 1997; Katz & Kahn, 1978; Schwartz & Bilsky, 1987).

A unique aspect to this research is the role of small business in the economy and the implications that the LMX exchange has for small business leaders to immediately improve the overall effectiveness of their operation. Small business challenges were reviewed in the literature and in the context of leadership overall (Davidson, 1989; Delmar, 1996; Gundry & Welsch, 2001; Harris & Arendt, 1988; Kotey & Slade, 2005; Wiklund, Davidson, & Delmar, 2003).

Complexity Economics

A discussion of economics is vital to an understanding about economic development. Complexity theory involves business/economic development ideas pertaining to the ability of entrepreneurs to create wealth. To evaluate the creation of wealth, people need to have a clear idea of the concept of wealth. "To summarize 2.5 million years of economic history in brief: for a very, very, very long time not much happened; then all of a sudden, all hell broke loose. Over 97% of humanity's wealth was created in just the last 1% of our history," (Beinhocker, 2007, p. 11).

Smith (2003) provided an early discussion on the topic in Wealth of Nations, suggesting that wealth is created through the process of people harvesting raw materials from their environment, and by the sweat of their brow, transforming raw material into something people want and need, thereby creating value. Smith also surmised that the allocation of wealth and resources is driven by specialization and, consequently, through trade. Beinhocker (2007) described Smith as an ancestor of traditional economics promoting the law of supply and demand that assumed market equilibrium is a given singular event. Over the next 200 years, traditional economists expanded the discussion of supply and demand and ultimately, the effect of price on a consumer's utility of choice. One problem that emerged was that the understanding of traditional economics did not allow for irrational choices by flawed people for unpredictable reasons, and as a result, the opportunity to gain a realistic view of the why behind the what was lost (Beinhocker, 2007).

Beinhocker (2007) described a blending of three key activities including physical technology as it pertains to things; social technology, as people are organized for tasks; and business design, which is the process of combining the two in order to provide products and services. As a result, an adaptive process emerged that was very dynamic and always evolving; thereby, creating the basis for complexity economics (CE) and the theory that an economy is an evolutionary system. CE extends beyond traditional economics seeking the value of a tangible item to a new dimension seeking to understand why choices are made.

Beinhocker (2007) credibly cited a number of historical, traditional economists including Smith, Gossen, Walras, Poinsot, Pareto, and Samuelson, and emerging contemporary researchers including Schumpeter, Popper, Kirman, Mirowski, Epstein, Axtell, Sterman, Simon, March, Cyert, Kahneman and Tversky. It is important to note because many current traditional theorists have difficulty recognizing CE theory. The collective journey of the distinguished cohort of economists has led to the creation of behavioral economics, which Beinhocker credited to Slovic, Camerer, Roth, Selten, Thaler, Lowenstein, Rabin, Prelec, Gintis, Fehr, Kagel, and V. Smith. Synergy from the process has produced a holistic blend of social science, mathematics, and information technology, supplementing behavioral economics and giving rise to the notion of complexity economics.

The adaptive process also became integrated with the rapidly innovative fields of gaming theory, cellular automata, and information technology.

According to Beinhocker (2007) a historical review of economic data demonstrates that the tenets of traditional economics, such as supply and demand, one price, equilibrium, and random walks, are not absolute and marginal at best and in contrast, complexity economists endorse "satisficing," the idea that real people are fallible and biased, making choices that are good enough based on the moment as opposed to the absolute best (Beinhocker, 2007).

Beinhocker (2007) indicated that the process of business development, or the creation of wealth, is cultivated and nurtured by a "pattern of matter, energy, and/or information, if the following three conditions are jointly met" (p. 303). Beinhocker listed these conditions as:

1. **Irreversibility**. All value-creating economic transformations and transactions are thermodynamically irreversible.

2. **Entropy.** All value-creating economic transformations and transactions reduce entropy locally within the economic system, while increasing entropy globally.

3. **Fitness.** All value-creating economic transformations and transactions produce artifacts and or actions that are fit for human purposes. (p. 303)

The value system is reinforced by economic development practitioners (Edward Lowe Foundation, 2010a, 2010b; Gibbons, 2010; Gibbons & Lange, 2010) who advocated a review and discussion of Beinhocker's (2007) research because it provided a primary theoretical foundation to the goal of wealth creation and business/community development by cultivating innovation and entrepreneurship.

The pattern of matter, energy, and information (Beinhocker, 2007) has been found throughout the evolution of commerce and business development. "Economists study the production, distribution, and consumption of goods and services. Students of organizational behavior share the economist's interest in areas such as labor market dynamics, productivity, human resource planning and forecasting, and cost-benefit analysis" (Griffin & Moorhead, 2010, p. 13). The process naturally fits into research studies of LMX theory and the choices leaders and followers make along the way, the impact of which directly benefits or hurts the individual and the enterprise (Graen, Dansereau, Minami & Cashman, 1975). The process of choice, chance, and change within complexity economics (Beinhocker, 2007) is congruent with the small business owner's choice of which followers will be in the in-group and which will be in the out-group, based on the behaviors and values the leader perceives followers possess.

Entrepreneurship and Innovation

Beinhocker (2007) provided an overview of economics history progressing from the earliest days of hunter-gatherers struggling to survive, to the advent of global manufacturers seeking to balance supply chains serving diverse global markets.

One powerful metaphor involved Beinhocker's comparison of Maasi tribesmen measuring wealth based on size of one's cattle herd to the most advanced technologists that create wealth from the context of a virtual domain. Regardless of the circumstance, entrepreneurship and innovation are hallmarks of economic development. In the context of complexity economics, the evolution of the marketplace needs entrepreneurs and tinkerers at all levels of an organization, and in all facets of a community.

The challenge is that people with basic needs, wants, and desires will consider, pursue, and acquire solutions that best meet their goals at a particular time, subject to those constraints they accept as reality at that moment. Entrepreneurship drives economic development followed by innovation and the "gales of creative destruction" acting as the primary tools that sustain revitalization (Beinhocker, 2007, p. 40). Sobel (2006) traced the definition of entrepreneurship from the 13th century

French verb entreprendre, meaning "to do something or to undertake" (p. 2). Sobel found the word progressed to entrepreneur, or "someone who undertakes a business venture" (p. 2), in the 16th century. Sobel recognized Cantillon for labeling entrepreneurs as those who bore personal financial risk for venture creation; Say, who said entrepreneurs create value by shifting resources; and Mill, for describing entrepreneurs as those who assume business risk and management in contrast to owners or shareholders who may assume financial risk but do not actively engages in daily management.

Sobel (2006) credited Schumpeter for the idea of entrepreneurs as innovators using the process of "creative destruction," and Kirzner, who described entrepreneurship as a discovery process leading to new profit opportunities that disappear once competition begins (p. 2). Sobel recommended the best way to promote entrepreneurship to be vesting in reformed government policies that create an environment in which entrepreneurs can be nurtured and flourish, thereby creating wealth. The idea is used to link into the view of economic development leaders who believe that the time correct for changes in public policy, but leaves open the question as to how a community can grow entrepreneurs.

Gartner (1989) offered a critique of researchers studying entrepreneurial traits and characteristics and found the researchers focus on two simple approaches as their theoretical foundation: "ideas about the differences between entrepreneurs and non-entrepreneurs and ideas about the difference among types of entrepreneurs" (p. 29). Gartner recommended that researchers clearly spell out the traits and characteristics that produce entrepreneurship, exercise care in the selection of individuals for study, and think carefully about the research methodology to be selected and followed.

Drucker (1985) suggested entrepreneurship is more than a list of personality traits that can be readily taught, advocating instead that entrepreneurs should be examined in a context of practice and not personality. Practice, process, and preferences are another way to examine behavior. Pillis and Reardon (2007) suggested a listing of entrepreneurial traits such as achievement motivation, risk, and ambiguity tolerance, and locus of control/personal efficacy, which they believed, could be taught, and emulated.

Drucker (1985) emphasized innovation as an essential component of entrepreneurial behavior, the practice of entrepreneurship, and strategies for leveraging change in the marketplace. While Drucker defined innovation as change creating new levels of performance, the implication was that change, innovation, and entrepreneurship are all elements of one dynamic process collectively, and are always in a state of flux. Gartner (1988) compared entrepreneurial traits to entrepreneurial behaviors, stating that entrepreneurs are like baseball players. "A baseball player is not something one is, it is something one does. Entrepreneurs, like baseball players, are identified by a set of behaviors which link them to organization creation" (p.58, 62). Gartner (1989) suggested entrepreneurship is the activity of venture creation, and once the act of creativity is over entrepreneurship ends.

Drucker's (1985) integration of innovation and entrepreneurship has been noted by several scholars, including Pearce, Marciariello, and Yamawaki (2010) who credited Drucker's advocacy for social sector innovation for giving rise to "social entrepreneurship," (Pearce et al., 2010, p. 124). In an attempt to clarify the two activities,

Gartner (1985a) suggested "entrepreneurship (organization creation) is a solution to those situations which need organizing, while innovation is a solution to those situations that need something new" (p.175). Sherwood (2002) stated that "bringing a new idea to full fruition, so that something actually happens, requires much more work than just having the idea in the first place," (p. 6).

Currently, "social entrepreneurs are being championed as change agents for society while business entrepreneurs are launching and creating new industries and ventures because of Drucker"(Pearce et al., 2010, p. 124). One role model for social entrepreneurs is Bill Drayton, chief executive officer (CEO) of Ashoka. Drayton demonstrated "visionary strategies on service, competitiveness, network building, partnerships, and community engagement" while he managed organizational change (Cordello, 2011, para. 1). The observation is reinforced by researchers examining entrepreneurial breadth and depth in rural versus urban settings (Low et al., 2005).

Hisrich, Peters and Shepherd (2008) clearly distinguished entrepreneurship and innovation as distinctive events. History has shown effectively several examples of gifted inventors/innovators who are not entrepreneurs, and, in reverse, where talented entrepreneurs are not inventors. Entrepreneurs strive to discover ideas for the marketplace, driven by the associated risk and rewards. In contrast, a backroom tinkerer/inventor seeks solutions to a problem and once solved, move on to the next challenge. Innovation is "the key to the economic development of any company, region of a country, or country itself. Inventions and innovation are the building blocks of the future of any economic unit," (Hisrich et al., 2008, p. 148).

Loewe and Dominiquini (2006) suggested company leaders foster core innovation competencies as a journey to become serial innovators. Loewe and Dominiquini advocated three essential paradigms, "don't just treat the symptoms, don't only act on one root cause, and don't blindly copy best practices," (p. 24). Acs, Braunerhjelm, Audretsch, and Carlsson (2009) cite four essential elements to building a systemic innovation culture, (a) leadership and organization, (b) culture and values, (c) people and skills, and (d) processes and tools. All of these activities demand visioning, collaboration, knowledge spillover, and access to resources and tools that nurture ideation (Acs et al., 2009, p. 15-18).

Since 2001, The Organization for Economic Cooperation and Development (OECD) has endorsed a new paradigm for regional growth that recommends pursuing three things simultaneously, "encourage regional critical mass by acting regionally to compete globally, prioritize investments in public goods and services to unlock a region's economic potential, and spur innovation to transform a region's economy," (Drabenstott & Moore, 2010, p. 42). New venture creation is used to balance four essential elements including (a) environment, (b) individuals, (c) organization, and (d) process.

Consequently, a kaleidoscope of diversity demonstrating new-venture-creation is unique, complex, and variable (Gartner, 1988). Katz and Gartner (1988) examined emerging organizations through an analysis of "four major properties: (a) intentionality, (b) resources, (c) boundary, and (d) exchange; properties that can be an effective tool used by researchers to distinguish between pre-organizations and existing organizations" (p. 429). This distinction is important because little is known or understood about pre-organizations that fail to launch or never make it to their first anniversary, a population rarely reported or documented, and known as the "near-misses" (Delmar & Shane, 2004, p. 392).

Low et al. (2005) provided a diverse, contemporary view of entrepreneurs, suggesting many begin their journey as self-employed and/or part-time owner-managers. The observation is significant because it recognized that some entrepreneurs "start their own business to fulfill a dream or follow a chosen lifestyle. Many lifestyle entrepreneurs benefit their community by enhancing the local quality of life" (Low et al., p. 63), and in contrast, high-value entrepreneurs are "masters at identifying and exploiting assets, and focus on "creating wealth, income, and jobs," (Low et al., p. 63).

Holistically, competency models are conceptual frameworks used to define behavioral knowledge, skills, and competencies that people need in a specific activity to perform effectively. Careeronestop.org is a website dedicated to the collection of competency model theory, and is home for the Ennis (2008) entrepreneurship competency model, shown in Appendix E, depicting a progressive collection of competencies ranging upward from personal effectiveness competencies, academic competencies, workplace competencies, entrepreneurship and technical competencies, occupation-specific knowledge areas, occupation-specific technical competencies, and occupation-specific requirements (Ennis, 2008). LMX theorists developed a wide path across the entire entrepreneurship model.

Ács and Varga (2005) documented the way entrepreneurs recognize knowledge spillover, facilitate innovation, and provide critical mass to technological change, thereby creating future markets for new goods and services. Acs and Varga suggested the volatility of the process is dynamic, and the movement of entrepreneurs into and out of rapidly evolving markets is sustained by entrepreneurial discovery, "a process of knowledge spillover where knowledge is a non-rival good" (p. 325). This means the one who discovers the knowledge may not be the one who exploits it. For example, the knowledge of this research study will benefit others beyond the immediate reach of the study (Acs et al., 2009).

The overview of entrepreneurship and innovation began with examples of Maasi tribesmen and virtual technologists. Regardless of the circumstance, access to information is vital to the ability of entrepreneurs to thrive and survive. Entrepreneurs who drive economic development are contingent on innovation, which is proportional to the quality of available information. "Information on its own can be worthless.

Knowledge on the other hand is information that is useful, that we can do something with, that is fit for some purpose. Wealth is knowledge, and its origin is evolution" (Beinhocker, 2007, p. 317-318).

Leadership

For decades, scholars have studied the phenomenon of leadership and published their findings in a wide variety of material.

The study of leadership rivals in age the emergence of civilization, which shaped its leaders as much as it was shaped by them. From its infancy, the study of history has been the study of leaders, what they did, and why they did it. (Bass, 1990a, p. 3)

The science of leadership has evolved over time from thorough studies of ancient civilization through modern culture, with the quest for understanding how leadership functions being as vital in modern society as it was thousands of years ago (Beckerleg, 2002; Burns, 2003; Enzenauer, 2004; Owen, 2000; Paul et al., 2002).

Enzenauer (2004) suggested that historical highlights such as the journals of military figures like Xenon, a military general and historian, continue to provide a solid foundation for understanding why effective leadership is vital. Xenon was a warrior, but his uncanny understanding of human psychology continues to be cited in numerous modern leadership theories and practices. Other historical figures considered to be influential are: Chinese philosopher and sage La-Tzu, who wrote the TaoTe Ching (How Things Work) in the 6th century; Niccolo Machiavelli, who wrote The Prince over 500 years ago (Callanan, 2004), and German philosopher Hegel, who in the 1800s, pondered leadership and the natural consequence of followership at the same time (Owen, 2000).

The discourses have been used to create vigorous discussions over rudimentary definitions of leader competency and what leaders actually do by Drath and Palus (1994), Katz and Kahn (1978), and Rauch and Behling (1984).

While many scholars focused on semantics and rhetoric, their collective effort consistently has caused two primary questions: First, can a leader be a manager at the same time, or is each role distinct? Second, how many leaders or managers can an enterprise have at the same time? Contemporary researchers of leader-member exchange theory have advanced the discussion by concentrating on the dyadic relationship between leader and follower as a process to be studied, defined, and understood more clearly (Deckert, 2007).

According to Fagiano (1997) and Robinson (1999), leadership and management are distinct, portraying different functional characteristics unique to each company setting. While some company officials empower leadership in the CEO and designate other employees lower in the organizational chart as a manager, officials at othercompanies may empower leadership in the board of directors. In contrast, leaders in smaller companies elevate the discussion due the smaller size of the company and the resulting pressure for the same person to lead and manage simultaneously (Kotter, 1997, 2000, 2006).

It is likely the owner or top manager may be the obvious administrative authority, yet the practice of leadership may clearly flow from management staffers close to or on the production floor. Sharma (1997) reinforced the idea by stating that management and leadership functions can be carried out by a number of individuals simultaneously across multiple levels of the organization. The idea is used to promote the view that effective managers embody effective leadership techniques, and as a result, leaders can be found across all levels of the organization, not just at the top. While a manager may not actually supervise someone, those who do are tasked with understanding why team members will follow a manager, and whether a manager is effective in the craft of leadership. "The essence of leadership is followership and that without followers there can be no leaders" (Collinson, 2001, p. 179).

Followership

While themes of management and leadership have thousands of titles, meaningful work on the science of followership has been limited (Johnson, 2003; Lundin & Lancaster, 1990; Rusher, 2005). To lead one must have followers, as Bennis (2009) concluded, "great leaders and followers are always engaged in a creative collaboration…the days when a single individual, however gifted, can solve our problems are long gone. We need groups of talented people to tackle them," (p. xxiv-xxv).

Bennis (2009) outlined four vital traits leaders demonstrate: "(a) engagement, (b) distinctive voice, (c) integrity, and (d) adaptive capacity, all of which show a strategic recognition of the high quality dyadic relationship followers can enjoy with leaders" (p. 375-386). Gilbert (1985) suggested effective leader-follower skills could be used to measure the success or failure of the relationship. Collinson (2006) emphasized, "the identities of followers and leaders are frequently a condition and consequence of one another," (p. 187).

Rosenau (2004) proposed, "It follows that the dynamics of leadership are intimately and inextricably tied up with followership" (p. 16). Leaders with conventional wisdom have long acknowledged that followers can make or break leaders and organizations (Collinson, 2006). Traditional educators and trainers focus solely on the top-down role of managers as leaders and how they steer the organization to success.

While the role of the leader should not be understated in the quest for the vision and mission of the enterprise, followers' contributions and sacrifices are often overlooked (Bennis, 1996, 1999, 2005, 2009). Contemporary researchers have focused on the role of followership as a valuable dynamic that strategically contributes to the likelihood of any organization's success (Deckert, 2007; Dixon & Westbrook, 2003; Rosenau, 2004; Stewart, 2003). The resulting effort has stimulated vigorous discussion concerning what a follower is or does, and in defining attributes of effective followers.

Meilinger (1994) identified nine essential activities used by effective followers to achieve success for the leader, the organization, and themselves, as shown in Table 1. Solvoy (2005) reinforced the idea by the list of eight behaviors exhibiting goodfollowership (see Table 2). While both scholars addressed the same idea, each presented a slightly different perspective on the theory of followership activity and the traits that define effective followers. Each idea is presented side-by-side for comparison purposes.

Table 2.1

Meilinger's (1994) Activities Defining Good Followership

1. Don't blame your boss for unpopular decisions; your job is to support it, not undermine it.
2. Fight with your boss if necessary: but do it in private, avoid embarrassing situations, and never reveal to others what was discussed.
3. Make the decision, then run it past the boss; use your initiative.
4. Accepting responsibility, whenever it is offered.
5. Tell the truth and don't quibble; your boss will be giving advice up the chain of command based on what you said.
6. Do your homework; give your boss all the information needed to make a decision; anticipate possible questions.
7. When making a recommendation, remember who will probably have to implement it. This means you must know your own limitations and weaknesses as well as strengths.
8. Keep your boss informed of what's going on in the unit; people will be reluctant to tell him or her, their problems and successes. You should do it for them, and assume someone else will tell the boss about yours.
9. If you see a problem, fix it. Don't worry about who would have gotten the blame or now who gets the praise.

Note: Adapted from: "Ten Rules of Good Followership." By P. Meilinger, 1994, Military Review, 74(3), p. 32. Copyright 1994 by Military Review.

Table 2.2

Solovy's (2005) Activities Defining Good Followership

1. Self-management
2. Communication
3. Teamwork
4. Personal Development
5. Commitment
6. Credibility
7. Honesty
8. Courage

Note: *Adapted from "Small Business Economics: A Global Perspective by Z. J. Ace, 1992, Challenge 35(6), p. ??. Copyright 1992 by Challenge.*

While Meilinger (1994) and Solovy (2005) provide a framework used to define the best practices for good followership, the overall body of knowledge lacks any consensus on specific followership values and behaviors that small business leaders identify as strategic to their enterprise. Kelley (1992) provided a foundation for followership research and baseline studies by defining 15 attributes used to define exemplary followership. The Kelley followership model was based on the premise of individual thinking attributes such as independent critical, dependent critical, active, and passive. Each aspect is used to add substance to the notion of followership (see Table 3).

Table 2.3

Kelley's 15 Attributes for Exemplary Followership

1.	Think for themselves.
2.	Go above and beyond the job.
3.	Support the team and the leader.
4.	Focus on the goal.
5.	Do an exceptional job on critical path activities related to the goal.
6.	Take initiative on increasing their value to the organization.
7.	Realize they add value by being who they are, their experiences and ideals.
8.	Structure their daily work and day-to-day activities.
9.	See clearly how their job relates to the enterprise.
10.	Put themselves on the critical path toward accomplishment.
11.	Make sure the tasks they are to perform are on the critical path.
12.	Review their progress daily or weekly.
13.	Increase their scope of critical path activities.
14.	Develop additional expertise.
15.	Champion new ideas.

Note: Adapted from *The Power of Followership* by R. E. Kelley, 1992, p. 126-166. Copyright 1992 by Double Day.

While Deckert (2007) provided a baseline for the characteristics summarized in Tables 2.1, 2.2, and 2.3, Tri-States expanded it further and elevated the understanding of who makes up small businesses in rural areas, how leaders can better motivate followers, and the affect that age, gender, and industry have on LMX.

Leader-Member Exchange (LMX) Theory

Dansereau et al. (1975) and Graen et al. (1975) elevated academic discourse of leader-member-exchange (LMX) as it was formally introduced to the academic world in 1975. LMX Table 2.3 relationship between a leader and individual followers. Prior to the formal introduction of LMX theory, most researchers concentrated on detailed lists of competencies and traits of leaders' activity when leading and motivating followers. Like earlier researchers, LMX theorists did not tell leaders what to do or what not to do (Northouse, 2004). LMX theory is unique because it is used to emphasize the natural evolution of the dyadic relationship between leader-follower and recent research has suggested this linkage is affected by the identity each party possesses (Haslam & Platow, 2001).

Engle and Lord (1997) benchmarked the quality of leader-follower relationships by expanding on Duchon, Green, and Taber's (1986) recommendation that the manner in which leaders treat individual followers is unique to each individual relationship and driven by the quality of each distinct relationship. An increasing body of empirical research on LMX since its inception has sustained the premise (Sparrowe & Liden, 1997).

Therefore, LMX theorists challenged traditional leadership models by depicting a variety of different dyadic relationships unique to both individual followers and the leader they interact with, and driven by a number of factors affecting the quality of each relationship (Phillips & Bedeian, 1994). The list includes, but is not limited to: (a) job climate, (b) follower's performance, (c) employee commitment to the organization, and other minor variables (Graen & Uhl-Bien, 1991, 1995).

Graen, and Cashman's (1975) original LMX research introduced concepts of in-group and out-group as indicators of the quality of the leader-follower relationship. Graen and Cashman benchmarked and measured the relationship development process between 60 manager leaders and their respective followers. Individuals in a manager's in-group were rewarded with special benefits from their manager, which included increased opportunities for direct input, stronger loyalty bonds, and higher levels of overall support from the manager. Followers identified in the leader's out-group received no special benefits (Kunze, 2006)

Wilhelm, Herd, and Steiner's (1993) study of attribution conflict's effect on leader-member exchange reported that in-group members were viewed by their leader as more trustworthy and, as a result, were given increased levels of rewards, support, and interaction. Conversely, out-group members experienced less trust, and restricted interaction and support.

One challenge associated with the process of identifying in-groups and out-groups is the allegation that a cloud of perceived inequity or unfairness might be cast subsequently on the enterprise (Norton, Vandello & Darley, 2004). Scandura (1999) suggested that when a perceived inequity exists, it might influence the way potential employees choose future employment. Lee (1997) suggested the process of in-group favoritism might have resulted from limited resources, which forced leaders to be highly selective and take care of the followers they believe to be most valuable. Out-group members are not perceived as worthy of similar treatment.

The phenomenon of a leader's in-group is purported to symbolize a high quality dyadic relationship. Recent researchers have depicted the in-group and out-group labeling process as three phases of a relationship rather than a clear-cut definition (Graen & Uhl-Bien, 1995). The high quality dyadic relationship has been assumed by some to describe any of the three phases, which, according to Graen and Uhl-Bien (1995), include: (a) stranger, (b) acquaintance, and (c) mature. However, this perception may be viewed as premature since each stage of the leader-follower relationship has several characteristics.

For example, the stranger phase is predicated on formal interactions between leader and follower, and is, therefore, transactional in nature. According to Graen and Uhl-Bien (1991), leaders will only provide followers with what is minimally necessary to perform during this stage, and followers will behave as required. During the acquaintance phase, leaders and followers evolve from interacting as strangers to exhibiting a blend of formal and informal interaction, sharing more information and resources along the way, however Graen and Uhl-Bien (1991) cautioned that, while the phase mixes personal and work interests, interactions are still measured and test whether contributions are equitably returned.

The third step of the relationship is the mature phase (Graen & Uhl-Bien, 1991) which is characterized by leaders investing more freedom in followers, sharing a mutual respect and trust, and assigning followers more premium assignments. During this phase, both parties function at optimal levels of interaction (Ashkanasy & O'Connor, 1997). The high quality dyadic relationship at the mature phase is marked by a mutual recognition of equal influence, shared goals, and supportive behavior beyond formal job requirements (Duchon et al., 1986).

Additional features of an effective high quality dyadic relationship are marked by intense levels of information exchange, shared support, shared decision making, strong in-group rapport, and efficient win-win negotiations between each participant (Lee, 1997). When the follower enters the in-group, a high-quality dyadic relationship naturally develops. However, when a follower falls into the out-group, the relationship is more often defined as low quality. The members of the former group enjoy acting as confidantes to the leader, while the latter is downgraded to a stranger relationship (Duarte, Goodson, & Klich, 1994; Lee, 1997).

Dienisch and Liden (1986) stated that understanding how the leader-follower relationship develops is as important as understanding the functional attributes of the relationship itself. The process of frequent interaction, trust, respect, goal sharing, and well-being enhances the leader-follower relationship and is vested in the in-group.

According to Deckert (2007), there are three main dimensions to understanding how high quality relationships develop,

1. Contribution: the amount, direction, and quality of work-oriented activity each member puts forth towards the mutual goals of the leader and the follower.

2. Loyalty: the public support of the goals and personal character expressed by one member of the dyad for the other.

3. Affect: the mutual affection each member of the dyad has for each other based primarily on the interpersonal relationship that develops between the two individuals. (p. 40)

Dienesch and Liden (1986) recognized the potential for more influencing factors beyond the list of three essential dimensions. Liden and Maslyn (1998) made two significant improvements which included: (a) introduction of a fourth dimension of professional respect, and (b) modification and expansion of the loyalty dimension to recognize mutual trust between leader-follower, instead of a fifth dimension driven by trust alone. Liden and Maslyn described the fourth dimension as a "perception of the degree to which each member of the dyad has built a reputation, within and/or outside the organization, of excelling at his or her line of work," (p. 50). This collective body of research has identified four dimensions to leader-follower relationship building, and how it can evolve from a low-quality relationship into a high quality dyadic relationship.

Understanding how the value process works is vital to those in a dyadic relationship who want to take it to the next level (Deckert, 2007).

LMX is a descriptive model of leadership instead of a prescriptive model, which is used to define the best leadership practices (Northouse, 2004). LMX theorists prescribed how to become a better leader by focusing on the interaction and chemistry between leader and follower, and the mechanism by which the process creates in-groups and out-groups. This understanding adds value to leaders by increasing their process knowledge and adds value to followers by teaching them the behaviors a leader desires most (Dansereau et al., 1975). As a dynamic, this complexity is used to reinforce the theory that the individual roles of leader-follower are co-dependent and inseparable (Collinson, 2006).

Value-Behavior Relationship

Katz and Kahn (1978) helped pioneer the research of organizational effectiveness and excellence, portraying organizations as orderly systems where each participant is assigned a position driven by rigidly defined roles and expected behaviors unique to each individual. Their definition readily adapts to LMX studies of a leader-follower, and the benefit that comes from understanding the values and behaviors that leaders expect their followers to model. Consequently, once a follower can understand the environment they work in and the associated expectations of their leader, the likelihood of their relationship evolving from an out-group to the preferred status of an in-group will be optimized (Sparrowe & Liden, 1997). Ultimately, both parties will benefit and the organization overall will benefit (Erdogan et al., 2004; Fernandez & Hogan, 2002; Meglino, Ravlin, & Adkins, 1989; Schein, 1985).

The process of value congruence should not be assumed that theorists imply that leader-follower values must be identical. Each value can be used to benchmark values unique to each individual, yet still be mutually beneficial to the overall relationship as well. Jehn, Chadwick, and Thatcher (1997) suggested each member seek congruence to satisfy the other party. "Thus, value congruence is achieved when an individual within the workgroup exhibits the values (and associated behaviors) expected by others in accordance with the individual's process and function within the workgroup," (Deckert, 2007).

Payne (1988) believed the research of values expanded across the scholarly community and propelled the analysis of workplace values to new levels of understanding. As a result, workplace value congruence is strategic and beneficial to all parties. Diener, Larsen, and Emmons (1984) suggested value congruence leads to increased job effectiveness and happiness. Other scholars also claimed that value congruence is tantamount to increased job satisfaction (Chatman, 1989; George & Jones, 1996; Meglino et al., 1989; O'Reilly, Chatman, & Caldwell, 1991), enhanced organizational loyalty (Harris & Mossholder, 1996; Meglino et al., 1989; O'Reilley et al., 1991), constructive workplace attitudes (Posner, 1992), higher levels of optimism about the future of the enterprise (Harris & Mossholder, 1996), and lower negative costs associated with employee turnover and new employee orientation (Chatman, 1989).

Collectively, these observations substantiate a powerful testament to the benefit of value congruence between an individual and their coworkers (Posner, 2010). Another dimension to the discussion, beyond the importance of individual value congruence, is the affect congruence has on the enterprise. Rokeach (1973) set the standard for the understanding by demonstrating that a low-value-congruence employee functions with a decision-making baseline that may not be compatible with the needs of the organization. As a result, employee incongruence leads to ineffective employee cooperation and communication (Chatman & Barsade, 1995; Kalliath, Bluedorn, & Strube, 1999; Posner, Kouzes, & Schmidt, 1985). Schneider (1987) developed the attraction-selection-attrition (ASA) model researchers use (Cable & Judge, 1997; Judge & Bretz, 1992) to indicate whether an individual finds a company desirable when its organizational values are compatible with the individual's values. In addition, company leaders are more inclined to choose individuals whose values are compatible with the organization's (Adkins, Russell, & Werbel, 1994; Cable & Judge, 1997; Kristoff, 1996).

The ASA model is also used to show that when employee values and organizational values are incongruent, the probability of turnover is increased (Cable & Parsons, 2001; O'Reilly et al., 1991; Saks & Ashforth, 1997).

Defining Values

Rokeach (1973) is widely recognized for his seminal work on leader-follower behaviors and values. In addition, Rokeach's (1973) research is routinely cited by researchers examining the connections between outer actions (behavior) and motivations (values). This body of knowledge is a critical foundational component to understanding what behaviors and values leaders prefer followers to possess and demonstrate, as well as how each of these influence the nature of the leader-follower relationship.

When people possess one of three basic belief systems, (a) beliefs that things are capable simply of being either true or false, (b) situations where the object of the belief is perceived as good or bad, and (c) circumstances where the activity or action is perceived to be desirable or undesirable (Rokeach, 1973; Rokeach & Ball-Rokeach, 1988). Rokeach (1973) suggested that values are immersed in the third belief system and that a "value is an enduring belief that a specific mode of conduct (Instrumental) or end state of existence (Terminal) is personally or socially preferable to an opposite or converse mode of conduct or end-state of existence" (p. 5). Deckert (2007) accepted the Rokeach model as an essential foundational premise to the North Florida study, and the notion that values are descriptors of desirable or undesirable behaviors based on a ranking order unique to each individual. Ultimately, values shape each person's actions, attitudes, and choices.

Rokeach and Ball-Rokeach (1988) categorized values as either instrumental or terminal. The terminal values show the desired end-states of each individual, and which goals are more important than others. Deckert (2007) focused only on instrumental values because the research was regarding only on those behaviors and modes of conduct leaders prefer followers demonstrate. Rokeach and Ball-Rokeach (1988) framed instrumental values as one of two distinct subsets: moral values or competence values.

Moral values are used to imply a personal focus for the individual. When a value is violated, a person's conscience is challenged and moral guilt is produced. Competency values are embedded in job requirements, and violations stimulate a sense of personal shame and inadequacy. This strong connection between collectivism and organization citizen behavior was established by Moorman and Blakely (1995). Although each instrumental value provokes differing emotions, they are action-related and behavior-related, and do not represent end-state or terminal values. Thus, Deckert (2007) included both types of instrumental values in the original North Florida study.

Rokeach (1973) suggested that when individuals described their least important values, they assumed their viewpoint would be applied to others as well. Rokeach showed that assumption was not necessarily true and that rankings were unique to each individual based on a complex standard of value and behavior ranking. Rokeach determined that individuals may apply their value systems in three ways, (a) to both themselves and everyone else equally, (b) to themselves but not necessarily to others, and/or (c) more to everyone else than to themselves. The nature of the diverse complexity of this choice process led Deckert (2007) to focus exclusively on those values and associated behaviors a small business leader perceives as most important and least important for a follower to possess and demonstrate.

While Rokeach (1973) provided a starting point for LMX research, modern scholars have expanded the concept with newer ideas. For example, Schwartz and Bilsky (1987) suggested that individual values are those beliefs or concepts that apply to one's desired behavior and provide a benchmark for shaping selection and desired behavior choices. Schwartz and Bilsky (1987) expanded their idea with the observation that values can also be characterized as those general attitudes and trans-situational goals that guide individual behavior.

O'Reilly et al. (1991) described values as "internalized normative beliefs that can guide behavior" (p. 492), expanding on original work by O'Reilly and Chatman (1986). Homer and Kahles (1988) stated that a person's value system will dictate the order of the belief system, and as a result, it will dictate both the preferred instrumental values and the most important terminal values. The idea was supported by Feather (1995) who promoted the view that values lead to the formation of belief systems, desirable behaviors, and action plans. Consequently, the link between values, behavior, and choice is irrefutable.

Value-Behavior Dynamic

The body of knowledge clearly showed that a person's values act as essential determinants in shaping behavior (Blood, 1969; England, 1967; England & Lee, 1974; Homer & Kahles, 1988; Maierhofer, Griffin, & Sheehan, 2000; Meglino et al., 1989; Merrens & Garrett, 1975; Ravlin & Meglino, 1987; Rokeach, 1973). Chatman and Barsade (1995) advanced the understanding by noting that a person's value of cooperation drives the demonstration of cooperative behaviors.

When the element of teams is considered, the value of power guides team performance, shapes team perception and the team's interpretation of procedural rules (Fonne & Mhyre, 1996; Maierhofer, Griffin, & Sheehan, 2000). An individual's values of collectivism drives the level of citizenship behavior (Moorman & Blakely, 1995), and a person's value of workplace fairness is directly linked to the level of disciplinary activity in the individual's job setting (Judge & Martocchio, 1992). When all of the characteristics are considered collectively, a viable relationship between values and behavior at the individual level can be established. Deckert (2007) established that while there appeared to be a preponderance of research to support the view that a person's values define and influence behavior, some researchers offered a dissenting view by suggesting that a person's values and behaviors were not related (Homer & Kahles, 1988; Skinner, 1971; Williams, 1979), and that the two were not causally linked to choices made (Skinner, 1971). Williams (1979) acknowledged that, while such views were present, the body of evidence to support the view was not definitive. Consequently, the Tri-States study agrees with the primary premise of the Deckert (2007) that a person's values describe and influence individual behavior.

LMX and Values

Researchers have suggested that two people who think alike—or who share cognitive functioning—share similar values, use a common communications system, and interpret and process information similarly (Meglino et al., 1989; Rokeach, 1973). Extending the theory to a leader-follower relationship can help explain why clarity of others' role expectations will improve mutual understanding of common goals and their ability to predict each other's behaviors (Meglino et al., 1989; Schein, 1985). Another derived benefit is a measurable reduction in uncertainty and negativity, which is followed by better collaboration, job satisfaction, and organizational commitment (Deckert, 2007; Schein, 1985).

"Happy cows produce more milk and happy workers produce more everything," (Doman, 2011, p. 1). This Midwestern metaphor is especially true when the leader-follower relationship is based in a setting with high job satisfaction and organizational commitment (Fisher & Gitelson, 1983). Maierhofer, Griffin, and Sheehan (2000) demonstrated that congruent value systems yielded positive outcomes, elevated supervisor ratings of staff job performance (Becker, Billings, Eveleth, & Gilbert, 1996), optimized teamwork (O'Reilly & Chatman, 1986; Posner, 1992), raised the standard for ethical conduct (Posner et al., 1985) and dramatically reduced employee turnover (Meglino et al., 1989; O'Reilly et al., 1991).

The interplay between the way people think and the way they act is at the core of the discussion of human behavior. Why do people choose to act the way they do, and how do such choices affect the dynamics of the leader- follower relationship? Gilbert (1985) chronicled a list of 18 behaviors that leaders value most from followers. The vigorously debated Gilbert model has been used as a leadership formula for success.

While Gilbert's list was never intended to be all-inclusive and did not rank order-listed items, it does provide a starting point for LMX research. Another shortcoming of Gilbert's model was its failure to identify those follower values desired most by leaders. Ravlin and Meglino (1987) evaluated work behaviors most valued by individual employees, but did not analyze those items most valued by the leader. Likewise, participants were not challenged to rank the list in terms of those values they thought peer followers should emulate to be successful.

This body of research is used to suggest that value congruence is very beneficial to working relationships, which implies that high quality dyadic relationships can only be sustained by value congruence. Fernandez and Hogan (2002) stated that a leader-follower relationship is compromised and disintegrate when value congruence is absent or ineffective. Erdogan et al. (2004) took the concept further by demonstrating that value congruence absolutely improves the quality of leader-follower relationships.

A major premise of the Deckert (2007) study was the belief that mutual congruence between leader and follower is essential for understanding, collaboration, and support to occur. Chell and Tracey (2005) laid the groundwork for this idea when they demonstrated that value congruence could only be achieved when each individual displayed those values and behaviors one expected to see in the other. Followers could not meet the expectations of the leader if they had no idea what those expectations were.

While this may seem simplistic, there is a lack of research on the LMX dynamics small business leaders' desire most from their followers.

Small Business Challenges

When pundits and business commentators analyze business development and free enterprise, the token companies bantered about are often the big public corporations like GE, IBM, and Microsoft. The shortfall in that analysis was in the simple fact that, according to the officials of the U.S. Small Business Administration, small business leaders are the backbone of America's economic engine, making significantly larger contributions than the larger public corporations (Small Business Administration [SBA], 2006).

According to Rowden (2002), the creation of wealth and economic business development is driven by and dependent upon small business entrepreneurs who often adapt, innovate, and assimilate both on the fly and at a pace much faster than the larger public corporations, which tend to move more slowly and methodically. Small businesses have a significantly higher level of diversity and minority ownership opportunity than larger public corporations.

The Small Business Administration (SBA) Office of Advocacy officials most often use the benchmark of 500 or less employees to define a small business (Small Business Administration, 2006).

The definition can be confusing for novice researchers, because other sites within the SBA website also suggest numbers ranging as high 5,000 employees at businesses that cross state lines, so a clear, simple, standard would be helpful. In a holistic view, the Small Business Administration (2006) officials track and report all small business activity in the U.S. Table 4 shows the SBA's perspective on the domestic effect of small businesses, highlighting seven key contributions provided by the small enterprise (Deckert, 2007)

Table 2.4

Summary of Small Business Contributions

1. Represent 99.7% of all employees.
2. Employ half of all private sector employees.
3. Generate 60 to 80% of net new jobs annually over the last decade.
4. Create more than 50% of nonfarm private gross domestic product (GDP).
5. Supplied over 23% of the total value of federal prime contracts in FY 2003.
6. Produce 13 to 14 times more patents per employee than large.
7. Twice as likely as large firm patents to be among the 1%.

Source: Small Business Administration, (2006)

One important dynamic to understand about the entrepreneurs who run small businesses is what motivates them. In a study of mainstream economic literature, Wiklund et al. (2003) discovered a common stereotype claiming wealth to be the main motivator. However, Wiklund et al. also noted that a growing number of contemporary researchers are proving this stereotype inaccurate. Evidence now classifies small business owners into several categories: (a) high value entrepreneurs, (b) social entrepreneurs, and (c) non-profit entrepreneurs (Davidson, 1989; Delmar, 1996; Gundry & Welsch, 2001; Storey, 1994). Increasingly, age, gender, and industry are also noteworthy (Heneman & Berkley, 1999).

A second dynamic is how a small business owner defines success. While the size of the enterprise directly influences the human and capital resources available, the likelihood of success is proportional to whether the business is a for-profit or a not-for-profit concern. According to Stavrou, Kleanthous, and Anastasiou (2005), "leader behavior is not only complex and multi-dimensional but also contingent upon the overall system in which leaders operate" (p. 188). Environment is a powerful factor in strategic business planning. Therefore, for smaller businesses, certain considerations such as resource availability will become more critical (Harris & Arendt, 1998).

Kotey and Slade (2005) evaluated the context of human resource management in small businesses, and observed that frequently, limited resources can restrict the structured management practices the enterprise may need to pursue. Thus, accountability and control may be compromised. This reality is in contrast to management practices at large public corporations that may be inclined to throw money at problems (Stavrou et al., 2005).

This led to a third dynamic dealing with operational control and the effect the internal workforce can have on the business (Deckert, 2007). It can be stated that managing the internal work force within a small business organization may be more complex and stressful than in a large organization, where the division of tasks and responsibilities are more narrowly defined. The operational span of control is the most important factor in keeping a company successful and growing (Drucker, 2004).

A fourth dynamic was founded in the fact that the work environment within a small business generally presents many restrictions on the type of work employees can focus on, frequently resulting in a work environment where employees are required to wear many hats and not simply focus on one particular function. Deckert (2007) noted the distinction based on research showing that the bigger the business, the bigger the division and differentiation of labor (Blau, 1970, 1972; Kotey & Slade, 2005).

Conversely, the smaller the business, the more likely it is that individual employees have to wear multiple hats, juggle several critical tasks, and run the risk of becoming overloaded and stressed (Harris & Arendt, 2005). Because the division and differentiation of labor is proportionately harder in smaller enterprises, the behaviors demonstrating flexibility, multitasking ability, and adaptability become more vital to leaders as they work with their followers.

A fifth dynamic is the context in which management evaluates or analyzes competitive intelligence or business research data. Traditional researchers tended to view all business operations through the same academic looking glass, ignoring how small businesses differ from larger counterparts. Haugh and Mckee (2004) noted the distinction:

> Current understanding informs us about management, marketing, strategy, human resource issues, and financial performance in the smaller firm. However, these measures only tell us about part of the organization, usually it is formal, objective, and visible aspects, and do not communicate a holistic view of what it is like to work in a small firm. (p. 377)

Knowledge of the interpersonal relationship dynamics in a small firm is critical to full appreciation of the leader-follower relationship in that setting. Often the layers between the leader and follower in a small business are few and more streamlined than they are in a big operation. Leader expectations for follower performance must be clearly understood and effectively demonstrated to assure success. A small business leader's personality can create informally structured settings and foster individual initiative that jointly leads to practical decision-making (Haugh & McKee, 2004).

Values Small Business Leaders Designate as Necessary to Succeed

The next logical step to clearly understanding LMX theory in the small business workplace is in knowing what leaders perceive the main barriers in the quest for success. Rogoff, Lee, and Suh (2004) identified internal and external factors for small businesses to overcome in order to survive and thrive (see Tables 5 and 6).

Table 2.5

Internal Factors for Small Businesses to Overcome

1. Work ethic: The desire and ability for those in the organization to work hard and to accomplish goals.
2. Knowledge: Those in the organization must have the appropriate level of knowledge, training, and experience to ensure the organization can be competitive and survive.
3. Dedication. The individuals in the organization must be clearly dedicated to wanting and working towards helping the organization to succeed.
4. Management skills. The organization must have adequate leadership and management in order for the organization to effectively utilize and direct its resources.
5. Marketing activities. The organization must engage in the proper types of marketing activities that will provide growth results for the company.
6. Product attributes. The organization must provide quality goods and/or services that consumer's desire.

Note: This table lists internal factors that must be overcome if a business is to be successful, according to small business leaders. Adapted from "Who Done It? Attributions by Entrepreneurs and Experts of the Factors that Cause and Impede Small Business Success" by E. Rogoff, M. Lee & D. Suh, 2004, Journal of Small Business Management, 42(4), pp. 364-377. Copyright 2004 by the Journal of Small Business Management.

Table 2.6

External Factors for Small Businesses to Overcome

1. Availability of financing: How easily and quickly can the firm attain financing when needed.
2. Economic conditions: The economic condition of the industry in which the firm operates.
3. Government regulations: The political and regulatory environment in which the firm operates.
4. Technology: The use and adoption of technology by the firm to gain advantage over competitors.
5. Environmental factors: Environmental regulations and restrictions that the organization must work under.

Note: This table lists internal factors that must be overcome if a business is to be successful, according to small business leaders. Adapted from "Who Done It? Attributions by Entrepreneurs and Experts of the Factors that Cause and Impede Small Business Success" by E. Rogoff, M. Lee & D. Suh, 2004, Journal of Small Business Management, 42(4), pp. 364-377. Copyright 2004 by the Journal of Small Business Management.

Rogoff et al. (2004) established internal factors to be the area that contributes most to company success, and found internal factors to be the area most small business leaders consider strategically vital to the company. As a result, leaders consider those followers who contribute most to the factors most valuable to the enterprise. In this context, individuals who contribute least are deemed less valuable. As a result, "one can make the assumption that the values and behaviors leaders most desire from their followers would be those values and behaviors most conducive to supporting the internal factors identified above" (Deckert, 2007, p. 42).

Kotey and Meredith (1997) found small business leaders who are entrepreneurial, proactive, and innovate are more prone to success. Kotey and Meredith suggested small business leaders who act like firefighters and react to circumstances are not as successful.

Translating the understanding to values and behaviors, the Kotey and Meredith found the following attributes to be most valued by leaders: (a) responsibility, (b) hard work, (c) honesty, (d) independence and loyalty, and (e) trust. Posner and Schmidt (1992) expanded the view in their study of key executives in large and small firms, finding the highest valued traits to be competence, dependability, honesty, open-mindedness, and long-term visioning.

Caution is advised to avoid assuming the identified traits from these studies are the same ones small business leaders value most in their followers. The studies cited (Kotey & Meredith 1970; Posner & Schmidt, 1992) are not follower specific, and do not concentrate on the traits most desired by business leaders. When measuring a firm's leadership success overall, a variety of external and internal factors must be evaluated to determine what dynamics are in play and the extent to which the leader-follower relationship embraces the key factors crucial to that setting (Posner, 2010).

An essential measurement of environmental workplace effectiveness is the recruitment and retention rates for a firm (Heneman & Berkley, 1999; Hornsby & Kuratko, 1990). High turnover and low retention rates are indicative of morale or supervision issues. Low turnover and high retention rates indicate a motivated team committed to the company mission. Regardless, value congruence leads to success, while incongruence can lead to serious organizational challenges (Judge & Bretz, 1992). It is strategically vital for the enterprise leaders to optimize recruitment and retention activities in order to achieve organizational excellence, an issue that has been a huge concern historically for small business leaders (Heneman & Berkley, 1999; Hornsby & Kuratko, 1990). Dalton and Todor (1979) showed the challenges that employee turnover cause for large and small enterprise leaders. George and Jones (1996) expanded on the challenges by showing the negative financial impact and the disruption to human resources and operations that voluntary turnover rates have on a business.

The cost of turnover is a debated, non-budgeted reality of running a business. Depending on the data source, the cost of turnover can range from 100 to 400% of the departing person's salary. Moore, Munzel, and Pfister (1998) estimated a 150% cost of turnover. Galbreath (2002) stated, "The true cost of turnover can be many, many times the amount you spend on recruiting activities. Estimates of the cost to replace supervisory, technical and management personnel run from 50 to several hundred percent of their salaries" (Para. 8-9). Actual costs can vary by job, industry, and business size. In companies with low retention rates, leaders can lose six figures a year, and smaller company leaders can experience an even greater impact (Williams, 2001).

Gatewood and Field (1987) highlighted the challenge to small business leaders, noting that smaller business leaders with limited resources use the owner-manager for recruitment and retention activity since small company leaders usually do not have a formal human resources (HR) department. Deckert (2007) noted that the use of effective screening tools would help the enterprise leaders hire smarter and not harder, ultimately reducing negative turnover costs. While Marlow and Patton (1993) established that effective human resource management is essential to a firm's success, research of the phenomenon in small business environments has been slow and very limited in scope (Hornsby & Kuratko, 1990). Typically, formal researchers of large firms have significantly overshadowed researchers of small firms, and great caution must be exercised to avoid assuming that data and lessons learned from large companies automatically apply to small businesses (Heneman, Tansky, & Camp, 2000; Hornsby & Kuratko, 2003).

Deckert (2007) noted the gap in the original North Florida research study, and found that the number of small business outnumber larger ones in total number of enterprises, total employment, and total number of new jobs created. Understanding of personnel behavior and values in small businesses remains limited, and researchers have been inconsistent (Hornsby & Kuratko, 2003). The call by Purcell (1993) for more small business research is still valid in 2011. This study responds to the challenge while being mindful that because of limited resources in small businesses, any knowledge the small business owner can gain in making high quality recruitment decisions will benefit the enterprise immediately.

Summary

In Chapter Two, several essential theories were explored and discussed. Complexity economics, entrepreneurship and innovation, leadership, followership, leader-member exchange theory (LMX), value-behavior relationships, defining values, value-behavior dynamics, LMX and values, Stage 2 small business challenges, and those values Stage 2 leaders indicated are areas necessary to succeed. This chapter also discussed the phenomenon of leadership and the way behaviors and values associated with followers have been overlooked until recently. Challenges presented by the lack of viable research associated with small businesses and the need for contemporary research in these areas is necessary and vital. A review of basic LMX theory was presented, from a holistic view of the journey to in-groups and out-groups, to the idea that the leader-follower model is a phased relationship journey to achieve the optimal high quality dyadic relationship phase, and ultimately improve the follower's chances for realizing several job benefits.

The literature review also indicated the nature of the relationship between values and behavioral outcomes, and how explicit values can be identified that offer optimal value-added benefits to the company. Likewise, the connection between LMX quality and values were discussed, and how the dynamic process affects the emerging leader-follower relationship. In addition, the challenges for small business owners were examined based on the significant contributions of small businesses to the U.S. economy in spite of significant recruitment and retention challenges, negative cost of turnover, and limited resources.

While Deckert (2007) added to the body of LMX knowledge with the focus on small businesses in North Florida, Tri-States builds on that foundation and expands the body of knowledge by the focused study of Stage 2 businesses in the three Dubuque Tri- State counties. Ultimately, benefits of this study will be used to better prepare business leaders to squarely face the current economic challenge head-on and seek creative solutions to survive and thrive (Atkinson & Andes, 2008).

The literature review was used to establish how individuals in a follower role could benefit with knowledge of how to become more effective within the leader-follower dynamic. The future benefit to small business owners who use LMX research to improve recruitment and retention challenges will be measurable, and will be enhanced by an understanding of what factors local business leaders' value in followers.

This understanding will create a leader's ideal follower model and add to the overall body of LMX knowledge for both individuals and organizational leaders alike.

CHAPTER THREE: METHODOLOGY

Research Design

Quantitative research strategically uses statistical tools (Reswick, 1994), quantitative methods, such as causal-comparative research analysis and comparison analysis (Simon & Francis, 2001), which allow for the use of established variables with numerical values that can be applied to diverse statistical methods and models (Bergsjo, 1999). Inu (1996) referred to the application of such techniques as a demonstration of the quantitative components of instruments, variables, and methods, as referenced by Reswick and Bergsjo.

Accepting the Rokeach (1973) premise that a person's behavior is driven by instrumental values and associated behaviors, in that context, it is therefore appropriate to study which instrumental values and associated behaviors small business leaders deem most important or least important for their followers to possess in an effort to sustain and drive the success of the company. Likewise, it is appropriate to examine what instrumental values and associated behaviors the same leaders deem most important or least important in their success as a leader. That was a premise behind the North Florida study (Deckert, 2007) and is a basis for Tri-States.

Tri-States focused on instrumental values and associated behaviors, examining the preferences of Stage 2 and Stage 3 company leaders (Edward Lowe Foundation, 2010) in the three Tri-State counties of Dubuque, IA; Grant, WI; and Jo Daviess, IL. Research concentrated on a rank ordering of 18 instrumental Rokeach Value Survey (RVS) traits and associated behaviors deemed most important and least important by the leader by their followers to contribute to the success of the enterprise. Likewise, the same leaders rank ordered the 18 instrumental RVS traits and associated behaviors in the context of the attributes they deem most important and least important to their personal success as a leader.

To maintain consistency with the North Florida study (Deckert, 2007), attention was focused on the top three and lowest three rankings which form the standard defining the most important and least important values. This analysis was not interested in causal relationships behind leader choices, but the instrumental values and associated behaviors chosen as most important and least important.

Tri-States will expand the existing body of knowledge by (a) providing leader-member exchange (LMX) data explicit to a rural geographic location in the identified Tri-States area; (b) linking the data to Stage 2 and Stage 3 companies as defined by the Edward Lowe Foundation (2011); and (c) benchmarking gender, age, and industry factors to determine the influence of such variables. Final analysis of survey data provides noteworthy comparisons in contrast to Deckert's (2007) study in North Florida because the same RVS survey instrument and quantitative methodology will be used.

The Rokeach Value Survey (RVS) instrumental values and associated behaviors Deckert (2007) adapted and administered (Rokeach, 1973; Rokeach & Ball-Rokeach, 1989) are discussed in Chapter Three. Even though Deckert did not provide comparisons to other geographic locations nor did he categorize age, gender, and industry datasets, his pioneering effort did provide a baseline for future LMX research. Deckert (2007) issued a call for additional research inviting other regions to consider similar studies, "to further understand how leaders in different regions of the U.S. may seek different values and behaviors from their followers" (p. 80). This study responds to that challenge.

Creswell (2009) specified that an effective quantitative research design follow project plans and a broader discussion of "specific methods of data collection, analysis and interpretation" (p. 3). While the Tri-States did not exactly replicate the original Deckert (2007) study, it does take inspiration from Deckert and closely emulates the quantitative methodology, instrumentation, and focus established by earlier scholars (Rokeach, & Ball-Rokeach, 1989; Braithwaite, 1994). This study can be reviewed to glean meaningful primary data for analysis, make geographic comparisons between Tri- States and North Florida, and adheres to the guiding principles established by Bergsjo (1999), Braithwaite (1994), Inu (1996), and Reswick (1994).

A major premise behind the LMX theory is that a person's values inspire and influence individual behavior (Rokeach, 1968). In that respect, Deckert (2007) concluded

It is important to investigate in which instrumental values small business leaders placed the most value, leading to a more accurate understanding of the actual followership behaviors leaders most desire. In seeking to determine the best way to measure instrumental values for the purposes of this research, it became apparent an instrument that could be used to identify and rank values was needed. (p. 49)

This understanding supported the goal of the Tri-States study to seek the most important and least important values as ranked by the leaders, which occurred once a statistical analysis of median and mean values was completed. The first four research questions as individual variables, are directly tied to this goal and because of the nature of their nonparametric design, each of the 18 values do not represent continuous variables; therefore, a computation of median and mean values for each item and each participant was produced.

Payne (1988) established there are several value instruments a researcher can select. Examples include "Allport, Vernon, and Lindsay's Study of Values (SV), England's Personal Value Questionnaire (PVQ), Rokeach's Value Survey (RVS), Rest's Defining Issues Test (DIT), and Edward's Preference Schedule [EPPS]" (Deckert, 2007, p. 51). Ultimately, the Rokeach Value Survey (RVS) is acknowledged for its desirable characteristics, widespread acceptance, and effectiveness in measuring personal and social values (Agle, Mitchell, & Sonnenfeld, 1999; Braithwaite & Law, 1985; Mueller & Wornhoff, 1990).

The integrity of the RVS is reinforced by its continued use across several academic research fields, and the inability of statisticians to refute the viability of its methods (Arsham, 2011; Braithwaite, 1994; McDonald, 2009; Ray, 1970).

In any research process, research seeking value information from a subject is not risk free. For example, open-ended questions that are too ambiguous allow participants to avoid focusing on key themes, while rigorous questions may be so intellectually demanding that participants are overwhelmed, contributing to high incompletion rates or shallow answers, either of which may yield invalid data (Fischoff, 1991). Participants asked to express views on anything more than short lists of specific questions, concerns, or issues, may not be able to articulate their thoughts (Creswell, 2009). Therefore, a solicitation process must be simple, non-threatening, and straightforward. The Tri-States study is designed to follow that approach; therefore, minimal risks are anticipated.

The RVS involves rank ordering of subject preferences and a quick turnaround time by participants (Braithwaite & Law, 1985). From education to psychology and business, the RVS has been applied in a variety of diverse ways, from measuring value structures for target populations (Rokeach, 1973; Rokeach & Ball-Rokeach, 1989) to the identification of differences between value systems of competing groups (Becker & Connor, 1981; Pitts & Woodside, 1983; Tetlock, 1986; Toler, 1975). A unique distinction of the RVS is the list of 36 traits, which Rokeach (1968) adapted from

Anderson's (1968) list that was obtained from 18,000 traits listed by Allport and Odbert (1936). As a result, a rich foundation emerged, grounded in commendable research over the years because the RVS "is one of the few instruments based on well-articulated value concepts," (Deckert, 2007, p. 51).

The distinction is noteworthy because researchers (Braithwaite & Law, 1985) have sought ways to improve on basic RVS value methodology, to the point of using weighted Likert scales, to no avail. Researchers using ongoing validation studies have not been able to undermine the reliability of the Rokeach Values Survey (Ray, 1970).

Research Questions and Hypotheses

In the Tri-States study, the same Rokeach Values survey used in North Florida (Deckert, 2007) was administered to Stage 2 and Stage 3 Tri-State leader participants inviting them to rank order a list of 18 instrumental RVS values and associated behaviors as directed. Each of Deckert's original two primary questions contained two variables; therefore, for clarity, the variables have been separated in this study to state clearly the first four research questions with an alternative hypothesis (Ha) and null hypothesis (H0) offered for each. Participant responses will be unique and subject to each person's preference based on their setting and culture. To be consistent with the Deckert (2007) study, the top three values ranked by each leader will be deemed most important, and the lowest three values ranked will be considered least important. In addition, age, gender and industry will also be evaluated to better understand any affect those variables may impose on results.

The last three research questions will be used to focus on these characteristics and because a mean score can be calculated for all top ranked values and all bottom ranked values, the means could be tested for relative strength against each of these three items using Spearman correlation methods. In that respect, this study may expand the body of knowledge beyond the original North Florida study.

As cited earlier, Appendix C illustrates the actual survey instrument used in the Tri-States study. The first four of seven primary research questions invite leader respondents to rank order the RVS instrumental values and associated behaviors in a particular way and each question is accompanied by a hypothesis and null hypothesis.

Participant leader responses are unique and subjective to each leader's preference based on their setting and culture. The final three of the seven research questions evaluate age, gender, and industry to understand better, how those variables might affect results.

Research Question 1 (RQ1). When asked to describe an ideal follower using a list of instrumental values and associated behaviors outlined in the Rokeach Value Survey [RVS] (Deckert, 2007), which instrumental values and associated behaviors will small business leaders rank most important for followers to possess?

H1$_0$. There is no difference in most important RVS instrumental values and associated behaviors as they relate to those ideal followers should possess.

H1a . There is a difference in most important RVS instrumental values and associated behaviors as they relate to those ideal followers should possess.

Research Question 2 (RQ2). When asked to describe an ideal follower using a list of instrumental values and associated behaviors outlined in the Rokeach Value Survey [RVS] (Deckert, 2007), which instrumental values and associated behaviors will small business leaders rank least important for followers to possess?

H2$_0$. There is no difference in least important RVS instrumental values and associated behaviors as they relate to those ideal followers should possess.

H2a . There is a difference in least important RVS instrumental values and associated behaviors as they relate to those ideal followers should possess.

Research Question 3 (RQ3). What are the most important RVS values and associated behaviors small business leaders should possess to perform and succeed as a leader?

H30 . There is no difference in most important RVS values and associated behaviors a leader should possess in order to succeed as a leader.

H3a . There is a difference in most important RVS values and associated behaviors a leader should possess in order to succeed as a leader.

Research Question 4 (RQ4). What are the least important RVS values and associated behaviors small business leaders should possess to succeed as a leader?

H40 . There is no difference in least important RVS leader values and associated behaviors a leader should possess in order to succeed as a leader.

H4a . There is a difference in least important RVS leader values and associated behaviors a leader should possess in order to succeed as a leader.

Research Question 5 (RQ5). Does age positively affect RVS rankings?

H50 . There is no difference in RVS values as ranked by leaders due to age.

H5a . There is a difference in RVS values as ranked by leaders due to age.

Research Question (RQ6). Does gender positively affect RVS rankings?

H60 . There is no difference in RVS values as ranked by leaders due to gender.

H6a . There is a difference in RVS values as ranked by leaders due to gender.

Research Question 7 (RQ7). Does industry positively affect RVS rankings?

H70 . There is no difference in RVS values as ranked by leaders due to industry.

H7a . There is a difference in RVS values as ranked by leaders due to industry.

Research Questions 1 through 4 are nonparametric in design and allow for the development of comparisons between Tri-States and the North Florida study. Research Questions 5 through 7 are unique to this study, parametric in design, and provide a new baseline for future research studies. The analysis of raw data is critical to the process and the accuracy and viability of the information is vital (Cone & Foster, 2006; Creswell, 2009), considerations that were critically examined during post survey data analysis.

Selection of Participants

The original North Florida Study (Deckert, 2007) chose business leaders across firms listed in the U.S. Small Business Administration's Central Contractor Registration (CCR) database, using simple random sampling after filters were applied. Each company consisted of 599 or fewer employees and had main operation located within North Florida. In 2007, 423,430 small businesses were listed in the national CCR database (Small Business Administration [SBA], 2006) but, after Deckert's three filters were applied, the sample population was reduced to 1,339 businesses across North Florida (Deckert, 2007). A shortfall with using the CCR database is that most small businesses are not government contractors; therefore, some business leaders do not register in the database and are not listed (Edward Lowe Foundation, 2009).

In Tri-States, a more stringent standard of defining small businesses was followed. The Edward Lowe Foundation (2011) performs customized research of entrepreneurial business operations across the USA and adapted Flamholtz and Randle's (2007) definitions for seven stages of business development into five steps: self-employed (sole proprietor), Stage 1 (2 – 9 employees), Stage 2 (10 – 99 employees), Stage 3 (100 - 499 employees), and Stage 4 (500 plus employees). This public data is available on the youreconomy.org website (Edward Lowe Foundation, 2011) and demonstrates that Stage 2 and Stage 3 segments are the largest job creators from 1992 through 2008. This makes Stage 2 and Stage 3 companies a critical research subject especially in the difficult economic times existing in 2012.

Across the Tri-States there are 15,639 total businesses and of that number, only eight employ 500 people or more (Edward Lowe Foundation, 2011). The remaining 15,139 are segmented into 65 Stage 3 businesses comprised of 100 to 499 employees, 1,214 Stage 2 businesses comprised of 10 to 99 employees, 8,063 Stage 1 businesses comprised of 2 to 9 employees, and 6,289 self-employed individuals, also known as sole proprietors (Edward Lowe Foundation, 2011; InfoUSA, 2011).

For the purposes of the Tri-States study, 277 public sector employers were removed from the 1,279 Stage 2 and Stage 3 companies, reducing the sample population to 1,002 private companies. Stage 2 and Stage 3 companies are significant because from 1992 through 2008 that segment across the Tri-States Market, specifically accounted for 51% of the total new jobs created. In contrast, Stage 4 companies only accounted for 7% of the new jobs. This reality provides a primary motivation behind this study focusing on that segment (Edward Lowe Foundation, 2009; Gibbons, 2010; InfoUSA, 2011).

This sample population is nearly as large as the North Florida study and comes from a smaller geographic area compared to Deckert's (2007). A challenge associated with using the CCR database is that only those small business owners who wish to do business with government agencies are listed because Federal and State regulation requires them to be registered with the CCR to bid on government contracts.

Therefore, the CCR is not a universal sampling of all small businesses. Companies at all stages, as defined in the Edward Lowe Foundation (2010a, 2011) database, include all businesses, CCR or not, for-profit and not-for-profit, public and privately owned (Edward Lowe Foundation, 2009; Gibbons, 2010; InfoUSA, 2011).

Consequently, in the Tri-States study, a sample population of 1,002 Stage 2 and Stage 3 Tri-State companies is significant because it clearly represents the segment creating the biggest job growth and expands on the original North Florida study (Deckert, 2007). In addition, the Tri-States study anticipates adding to the body of knowledge specifically by examining the correlation of age, gender, and industry data and how the factors affect the value ranking process.

Instrumentation

The Rokeach Value Survey (RVS) categorizes two sets of values with 18 individual traits or associated behaviors contained in each set. The philosophical basis behind RVS was first prescribed by Rokeach (1968), who stated that beliefs and attitudes are fundamentally connected to values. The RVS (Rokeach, 1973) portrays this methodology as terminal values, which point to the goals a person wants to achieve in his or her lifetime, and instrumental values, behaviors a person will implement to achieve the terminal values (See Table 7). Participants are asked to rank order a list of 18 items in order of personal importance.

Since 1968, the RVS has been used extensively and empirically by psychologists, sociologists, and market researchers (Johnston, 1995). Further, several attempts to downsize and streamline the original lists into more generic factors have not succeeded uniformly or consistently (Feather & Peay, 1975; Johnston, 1995).

Table 3.1

RVS Values, Traits and Behaviors

Terminal	Instrumental
True Friendship	Cheerfulness
Mature Love	Ambition
Self-Respect	Love
Happiness	Cleanliness
Inner Harmony	Self-Control
Equality	Capability
Freedom	Courage
Pleasure	Politeness
Social Recognition	Honesty
Wisdom	Imagination
Salvation	Independence
Family Security	Intellect
National Security	Broad-Mindedness
A Sense of Accomplishment	Logic
A World of Beauty	Obedience
A World at Peace	Helpfulness
A Comfortable Life	Responsibility
An Exciting Life	Forgiveness

Note: Terminal question: Rank order the 18 terminal values from the most important to the least important goals to achieve in your lifetime. Instrumental question: Rank order of the 18 instrumental values from the most important to the least important behaviors you will pursue in order to achieve your terminal value goals. Adapted from "The Nature of Human Values" by M. Rokeach, 1973, p. 26. Copyright 1973 by Free Press.

A compelling feature of the RVS is in the ability of the researcher to adapt or modify the RVS to meet the research objectives of a specific project; this feature and attribute is documented in the Creative Commons Attribution-ShareAlike 3.0 Unported License (Creative Commons Corporation, 2011) and posted on the Creative Commons Corporation Facebook® webpage for the RVS. The goal of the Creative Commons Corporation officials is to encourage as universal use and administration of the RVS as possible, assuming copyright control after Rokeach passed.

In the North Florida study, Deckert (2007) summarized how the RVS can be used effectively: One may use the Rokeach Value Survey to measure terminal values, instrumental values or both. Additionally, the instrument can measure such values using Likert scales or ordinal ranking (Rokeach & Ball-Rokeach, 1989). Rokeach and Ball-Rokeach also observed that one's priority of values could be more directly inferred from ranking the values rather than rating them. Thus, it was determined the ordinal ranking approach would have the better chance of achieving the most insight into the values, and subsequent behaviors, most desired by small business leaders of their followers. (p. 51)

Although researchers may use the RVS to study terminal and instrumental values, Deckert (2007) chose to concentrate on instrumental values and their associated behaviors, as shown by the 18 RVS instrumental values and associated descriptors (Fields, 2002) illustrated in the list Deckert adapted for use in the North Florida survey

1. Ambitious (hard-working, aspiring)

2. Broadminded (open-minded)

3. Capable (competent, effective)

4. Cheerful (lighthearted, joyful)

5. Clean (neat, tidy)

6. Courageous (standing up for your beliefs)

7. Forgiving (willing to pardon others)

8. Helpful (working for the welfare of others)

9. Honest (sincere truthful)

10. Imaginative (daring, creative)

11. Independent (self-reliant, self-sufficient)

12. Intellectual (intelligent, reflective)

13. Logical (consistent, rational)

14. Loving (affectionate, tender)

15. Obedient (dutiful, respectful)

16. Polite (courteous, well-mannered)

17. Responsible (dependable, reliable)

18. Self-controlled (restrained, self-disciplined) (Deckert, 2007, p. 56).

This list drove Deckert's primary research goals and formed the basis for this study's design as shown in the Tri-States RVS Survey Instrument (cited earlier as Appendix B). Leader participants were directed to rank order the same instrumental values list in two scenarios (Deckert, 2007). Scenario One was used to prioritize those values that the leaders deemed most important and least important for their followers to possess; Scenario Two was used to identified those instrumental values that the leaders perceived as most important or least important for them to possess as a successful leader. Both scenarios were germane to Deckert's (2007) primary purpose in the study and were achieved.

In the Tri-States study, this researcher had a similar strategic focus and area of inquiry with Deckert's (2007) study: What values and associated behaviors do Stage 2 and Stage 3 small business leaders across the Tri-States deem most important and least important for their employee-followers to possess for the enterprise to achieve success?

Likewise, what are the most important and least important values and associated behaviors the leaders believe they need to achieve possess and demonstrate as a successful leader? The research questions and hypotheses for this study reflect these areas of interest.

Sampling Protocol

Tri-States utilized a sample size calculator by Raosoft® (2011) with a 5% margin of error, a 95% confidence level, assumes a 50% response distribution and a population of 1,002. Consequently, the recommended sample size was 278. A sample size of 400 yields a confidence level of 99%, whereas a sample size of 214 yields a 90% confidence level. While population and sample size are noteworthy, the actual number of completed surveys produced by the research effort is critical.

In North Florida, the survey objective was to achieve a 5 to 10% completion rate to generate a targeted goal of 25 to 50 completed survey responses. However, Deckert (2007) found this extremely difficult to achieve:

> While most aspects of the study went smoothly, there was a low response rate (.012% with .009% useable) to the survey invitation email sent to potential participants. The low response rate resulted in a greatly increased reliance on direct solicitation of potential leadership participants by the researcher in order to achieve target response rates from small business leaders. As such, the final response rate of 29 participants exceeded the targeted minimum participant response rate of 25 and ultimately had to utilize extended direct solicitation methods to ultimately achieve their projected numbers. (p. 77)

Similar University of Wisconsin Platteville surveys targeted regional small businesses in the Tri-State area from 2007 through 2010 with a comparable 5 to 10% response goal and also fell short (Steinback, 2010). When considering the results of either study, while 14 to 28 completed surveys may satisfy minimal statistical standards for completed surveys (Cooper & Schindler, 2008) the Tri-States study wants to accomplish a level of statistical significance. Therefore, comparing N = 183, with the formula N = 50 + 8m (Tabachnick & Fidell, 2007), confirmed 183 cases as significantly greater than the calculated minimum value of N = 66, for two independent variables. This equation is for the minimum number of cases in a completely random binomial sample to approximate a standard binomial distribution. Tri-States aimed for a completed response goal of 66 to 183 cases in order to strive for significance.

To get there, the Tri-States study took the sampling population of 1,002 small business leaders across the Tri-States region and applied a simple random selection technique (Cooper & Schindler, 2003, 2008), picking every third company on an alphabetical list of all 1,002, until list of 278 targeted samples was achieved. At that point, a second tier was created by continuing to the end of the list and then starting the process over with the second line on the list and selecting every third company until an additional 200 companies populated the second tier of target companies. As the survey process proceeded, tier two was used to provide alternative replacements for no-responses, companies that have gone out of business or left the area, etc.

Time was of the essence in this study, so the principle investigator immediately utilized a direct solicitation working in order from the list of target companies, and provided each company with a packet of instructions directing them to the survey website. No interviews or direct contact with the ultimate survey participant took place.

Direct solicitation consisted of email, postal mail, phone calls, or site visits to deliver information packets. A back up contingency plan was utilized to achieve desired response rates. Local CPA firms, attorneys, trade associations, and chambers of commerce were contacted to make direct referrals to their clients and or members, who also happen to be on the list of 1002 companies.

Data Processing and Analysis

Survey leader participants were directed to the encrypted web-based site, managed by Survey Monkey®, and access was password protected and limited to one visit by a single participant once they have submitted their completed survey. Survey Monkey® provided for the secure and confidential control of centralized data (Verisign version 3 128-bit SSL). For security purposes, raw data was stored in an isolated database that only the researcher can access with the correct username and password (Survey Monkey, 2011).

Informed consent was clearly stated in all survey materials, and demonstrated in the online survey by the participant signifying their consent by hitting the submit survey button at the end of the survey. Each participant could clearly opt out at any time and from any page throughout the survey. Opt-outs will not count as submitted surveys. At no time was personal identifying information asked or collected. No human subjects were studied.

Permission for use of the RVS is shown in Appendix F, as provided by the copyright holder, Creative Commons (2011), Attribution-ShareAlike 3.0. Creative Commons has published the Rokeach Value Survey in Facebook® as a shareware document with the intent it be widely used and adapted as researchers see fit, provided copyright recognition and ownership is duly provided.

The use of Survey Monkey® ensured privacy and confidentiality for each point of contact or designee invited to participate and complete the survey. Opt-out options existed before and during the survey, up until the final submit button was selected by the participant. Guidelines were stated in the survey clarifying how the leader designation should be interpreted and applied before proceeding. Survey Monkey® protocol limited access to password protection. All Argosy University Internal Review Board (IRB) guidelines and protocols were applied.

Survey data was compiled by cases into Microsoft® Excel tables, segmenting rankings for each of the 18 values for each participant (Overton, 1997). A unique number identified each case. A table of values was constructed to facilitate calculating mean and median scores for each value. The top three scores yielded the three most important items, and the three bottom or least important item scores. Means, medians, and composite values for each instrumental value were computed by compiling each individual respondent's personal ranking of values. Ranking for each instrumental value was produced.

Finally, nonparametric testing was used to show significance of difference between the numbers of participants in the groups who scored below or above the mean or median (Deckert, 2007). Rokeach (1973) established the use of nonparametric testing as the primary test for statistical significance and endorsed the use of other tests of significance such as ANOVA, t-test, and the Kruskal-Wallis test, all of which were utilized in the original North Florida study (Deckert, 2007, p. 55).

Deckert (2007) was explicit in the rationale for using nonparametric testing because variables within the study were ordinal and interval measures could not be assumed. To be consistent with the North Florida study and to allow for meaningful comparisons of data with Tri-States, the top three and bottom three rankings in each category were be used a focal point of the analysis.

Once data was received and documented, a careful analysis of the final sample size and the appropriateness of running other tests, such as the Spearman correlation coefficient (r_s) could be determined. It is important to note that some researchers do not utilize Spearman in conjunction with Rokeach Value Surveys that use rank ordering

(Braithwaite, 1994; Gibbins & Walker, 1993). Arsham (2011) did not cite Spearmen as an option in the context of ordinal data that was rank ordered within the Rokeach Value Survey and Likert scales were not used. McDonald (2009) did not allow for the possibility of using Spearmen, and cautions,

you will rarely have enough data in your own data set to test the normality and homoscedasticity assumptions of regression and correlation; your decision about whether to do linear regression and correlation or Spearman rank correlation will usually depend on your prior knowledge of whether the variables are likely to meet the assumptions. (p. 1)

Once data was received and documented, a determination of the appropriate statistical tests and analysis was made. The expectation before the survey began, was that Spearman would not apply to the rank ordering of the Rokeach instrumental value data. Spearman's correlation was evaluated for use in analyzing the individual relationships between age, gender, industry of participant, and frequency of top pick.

However, demographic data for the following areas: (a) educational level, (b) years in small business leadership, (c) age, (d) gender, and (e) industry was measured against using Spearman's Rho once the means for the top three and bottom three items were determined. The relationship between the two was tested to see if they could be run against each demographic item as continuous variables. Once final data was collected and documented, a determination was made.

Assumptions

Although the RVS has been a survey tool for over four decades, some researchers claim the process of rank ordering terminal and instrumental values generate an ipsative measurement (Rankin & Grube, 1980). As a result, scholars have tested modified RVS tools that have yielded interval measurements of value importance (Miethe, 1985; Moore, 1975; Munson & Mcintyre, 1979; Rankin & Grube, 1980). Deckert (2007) addressed the debate directly and concluded

that subsequent analysis produced mixed results of the empirical comparisons between the ranking and rating data collection methods. Regardless of the controversy of measurement, the ordinal ranking method continues to be the method of choice of the value researcher. This method is seen as being the method that most accurately reflects the inherently comparative nature of values. (Kamakura & Mazzon, 1991, p.52)

Tri-States is consistent with North Florida in this context.

Limitations

Limitations include lingering uncertainty associated with the on-going recession and business owners' perceptions of the effect on business operations and the standardized RVSA instrument (Rokeach, 1973; Rokeach & Ball-Rokeach, 1989) as used in North Florida. Demographics were modified to collect data on age, gender, and industry, along with customized cover letters and distribution protocols to reflect local requirements and Argosy University IRB requirements.

Delimitations

Delimitations include the fact that the target sample survey was geographically confined to three Tri-State counties that include Dubuque, Grant, and Jo Daviess counties, and that the focus will be only on Stage 2 and Stage 3, private, for-profit companies. This survey only targeted small business leaders for the leader's perspective and the correlation of age, gender, and industry data as produced in the research.

Summary

Chapter 3 presented a detailed overview of the methodology associated with the Tri-States study and the quantitative research performed using an RVS tool adapted by Deckert (2007). Consistent with Deckert is an emphasis on better understanding the values and behaviors that small business leaders deem as most important and least important for their followers to possess to contribute to the success of the business. In addition, leaders were asked to also identify those same values that are most important and least important for them to possess as effective leaders for them to succeed in their roles.

The nature of participant demographics and the impact those values may have on ranking orders was discussed, along with parametric tests such as Spearman Correlation in that aspect of the statistical analysis. Deckert (2007) did not utilize Spearman's Rho in the original North Florida study and its possible use here could expand the body of knowledge.

Research design, seven research questions and accompanying hypotheses were reviewed. Population and sampling procedures were discussed as well as the selection process for determining the target population, survey instrumentation. sampling protocol, data processing and analysis. Expanded results, data, and statistical analysis are reported in Chapter 4, with subsequent conclusions and recommendations reported in Chapter 5.

CHAPTER FOUR: DATA ANALYSIS AND RESULTS

Introduction

Followership in the Tri-States recognized the premise that the science of management (Johnson, 2003; Lundin & Lancaster, 1990; Rusher, 2005) has historically emphasized theoretical leadership traits from a top-down perspective while ignoring the role of followers, which most people personally experience over the course of their professional careers (Dixon & Westbrook, 2003; Johnson, 2003). Tri-States also recognized Rokeach's (1973) premise that one's behavior is driven by instrumental values and associated behaviors.

In that context, it is therefore appropriate to study which instrumental values and associated behaviors small business leaders deem most important or least important for their followers to possess in an effort to sustain and drive the success of the company. Likewise, it is appropriate to examine what instrumental values and associated behaviors the same leaders deem most important or least important in their success as a leader.

That was a premise behind Deckert's Foundations of Followership in North Florida study (2007) and is a basis for the Followership in the Tri-States.

Participating small business leaders rank ordered 18 RVS instrumental values and associated behaviors, for two scenarios: 1) what values and associated behaviors did they deem most important and least important for employee-followers to possess for the enterprise to achieve success; and, 2) what are the most important and least important values and associated behaviors they believe are necessary for them to possess and demonstrate as a successful leader? Findings are reported below as data correlates to scenario one (SC1) and scenario two (SC2), and comparisons to Florida will be offered in Chapter Five.

Research Questions and Hypotheses

Seven research questions reflect this study from the perspective of small business leaders. The first four invite participant leader responses that are unique and subjective to each leader's preference based on their setting and culture. The final three evaluate age, gender, and industry, seeking to determine how those variables might affect results.

Each research question (RQ) is listed below with the corresponding null hypothesis (H0) and alternative hypothesis (Ha).

RQ1: When asked to describe an ideal follower using a list of instrumental values and associated behaviors outlined in the Rokeach Value Survey [RVS] (Deckert, 2007), which instrumental values and associated behaviors will small business leaders rank most important for followers to possess?

H1₀ : There is no difference in most important RVS instrumental values and associated behaviors as they relate to those ideal followers should possess.

H1a : There is a difference in most important RVS instrumental values and associated behaviors as they relate to those ideal followers should possess.

RQ2: When asked to describe an ideal follower using a list of instrumental values and associated behaviors outlined in the Rokeach Value Survey [RVS] (Deckert, 2007), which instrumental values and associated behaviors will small business leaders rank least important for followers to possess?

H2₀ : There is no difference in least important RVS instrumental values and associated behaviors as they relate to those ideal followers should possess.

H2a : There is a difference in least important RVS instrumental values and associated behaviors as they relate to those ideal followers should possess.

RQ3: What are the most important RVS values and associated behaviors small business leaders should possess to perform and succeed as a leader?

H3₀ : There is no difference in most important RVS values and associated behaviors a leader should possess in order to succeed as a leader.

H3a : There is a difference in most important RVS values and associated behaviors a leader should possess in order to succeed as a leader.

RQ4: What are the least important RVS values and associated behaviors small business leaders should possess to succeed as a leader?

H4₀ : There is no difference in least important RVS leader values and associated behaviors a leader should possess in order to succeed as a leader.

H4a : There is a difference in least important RVS leader values and associated behaviors a leader should possess in order to succeed as a leader.

RQ5: Does age positively affect RVS rankings?

H5₀ : There is no difference in RVS values as ranked by leaders due to age.

H5a : There is a difference in RVS values as ranked by leaders due to age.

RQ6: Does gender positively affect RVS rankings?

H6₀ : There is no difference in RVS values as ranked by leaders due to gender.

H6a : There is a difference in RVS values as ranked by leaders due to gender.

RQ7: Does industry positively affect RVS rankings?

H70 : There is no difference in RVS values as ranked by leaders due to industry.

H7a : There is a difference in RVS values as ranked by leaders due to industry.

The top three and bottom three choices in Scenario One and Scenario Two are documented and any identifiable differences are duly noted. The Statistical Package for the Social Sciences (SPSS) was used to code and tabulate scores collected from the survey. An excel spreadsheet was used to tally the raw scores for all 112 data sets for each of the 18 values rank ordered in Scenario One and again, in Scenario Two, which applied to RQ1, RQ2, RQ3 and RQ4.

The composite total score for each of the 18 values was computed and the mean and median average calculated. As a result, values were rank ordered apart from the alphabetical list and the top three and bottom three designated. Demographic statistics produced by Part One include count and percent statistics to profile participants. All research data produced was produced from the Tri-States LMX Survey 2012 (Table 4.1).

Table 4.1

Specified Design Components Related to the Seven Hypotheses

Hypothesis	Variable 1	Variable 2	Target	Statistics
H1	Most Important RVS		Ideal Followers	Descriptive
H2	Least Important RVS		Ideal Followers	Descriptive
H3	Most Important RVS		Leader Success	Descriptive
H4	Least Important RVS		Leader Success	Descriptive
H5	RVS Values	Age/Generation	Ideal Followers	Descriptive, ANOVA
H6	RVS Values	Gender	Ideal Followers	Descriptive, s-test
H7	RVS Values	Industry	Ideal Followers	Descriptive, ANOVA

Data Collection

Across the Tri-States area, 1,279 Stage 2 and Stage 3 small businesses were selected out of 15,639 total companies (Edward Lowe Foundation, 2011; InfoUSA, 2011). Two hundred seventy-seven public sector employers were removed, reducing the sample population to 1,002 private companies. A sample size of 278 (Raosoft®, 2011) was targeted with a goal of 66 to 183 completed surveys for statistical significance (Tabachnick & Fidell, 2007). Simple random selection techniques (Cooper & Schindler, 2003, 2008), identified 278 primary targeted samples along with a second tier of an additional 200 companies. A second tier was designed to be used as insurance to boost the completed survey count to a level of significance equal to or greater than 100.

The initial fourteen days of direct solicitation consisted of 246 face-to-face visits and 32 emails, yielding 63 responses and 60 completed surveys for a 21.6 percent response rate. Although the minimal threshold of significance was nearly realized, over the next seven days another 75 companies were solicited face-to-face and six by email, increasing the direct solicitation to 359. As a result, participation increased to 107 responses and 101 completions, for a 28.1 percent response rate. On the twenty-first day direct solicitation ended and the survey closed three days later. Eleven stragglers in the pipeline drove final numbers up to 118 total responses and 112 total completions, driving upward the overall response rate to 32.9 percent and the overall completion rate to 31.2 percent.

No interviews or direct contact with the ultimate survey participant took place. The principal investigator manually entered eight surveys on behalf of respondents who did not have web access and wanted to participate. A total of six opted-out of the survey after starting it. Three indicated by email to the principle investigator that they no longer met survey requirements and one indicated they could not rank order the values listed.

The other two are unknown. None of the six were included in collected data for Demographics, Scenario One, or Scenario Two. Local CPA firms, larger Chambers of Commerce, and Economic Development offices were not helpful due to internal policies restricting third party endorsements. It appeared to the principal investigator that smaller enterprises were more enthusiastic and eager to participate, and the largest settings were the most reluctant and hesitant due to internal policies or concerns.

Demographics

The demographics section, Part One of Tri-States LMX Survey 2012, asked participants to respond to eight questions. Question one required a unique four digit security code to officially enter the survey. The six respondents that entered but did not complete the survey were excluded from data analysis. Question two sought county location with the following percentage distribution revealed: Dubuque, 61.9; Grant, 19.5; Jo Daviess, 2.5; and rather not say, 16.1.

Appendix G provides six demographic data frequency tables summarizing survey information associated with demographic questions three through eight. Question three (AppendixG-1) asked respondents about NAICS industry and 21.6 percent work in Retail Trade, 11.7 percent work in Accommodations & Food Services, and 10.8 percent work in Health Care & Social Assistance – forming the top three industries which combined, account for 42.8 percent of the total sample. The sample was not large enough to generate meaningful information beyond the top three industries represented.

Question four (Appendix G-2) collected Education data, finding the following percentage distribution by level attained: 0.9 with no HS diploma, 24.1 with a HS Diploma, 12.5 with an Associate's degree, 40.2 with a Bachelor's, 9.8 with a Master's, and 12.5 with a Doctorate. Question five (Appendix G-3) measured total years in a small business leadership position with the following percentage distribution: 21.4 reported 21 years plus, 6 – 10- years, 21.4 have 1 – 5 years, and 10.7 reported less than one year of experience.

Question six (Appendix G-4) sought age information adapted to conform to generational clusters representative of Baby Boomers (36.6 percent), Gen X (36.4 percent), and Gen Y (25.0%). Generational age groupings were based on Edward Lowe Foundation (2011) data defining Boomers as age 50 plus, Gen X as age 30 to 49, and Gen Y as age 18 to 29, with distinct generational characteristics that will be addressed further in Chapter Five.

Question seven (Appendix G-5) measured gender, with 38.2 percent Female and 61.8 percent Male. Ethnicity of respondents was captured in Question 8 (Appendix G-6) with 95.5 percent Caucasian, 1.8 percent Other, 1.8 percent Rather Not Say, and 0.9 percent African American. While Age, Gender and Industry are unique to this study, the other demographic questions will be discussed in Chapter Five in the context of a comparison to North Florida (Deckert, 2007).

Data Analysis

Research Question 1 Findings

Table 4.2 displays the differences between the top three ranked RVS values for an "ideal employee." Top three rankings were defined by cumulative percentage by adding up frequency of responses for rank 1, 2, and 3 for a specified RVS value. Total percentage value was then calculated to determine rank order. As indicated, leaders ranked the top three RVS values as Ambitious, honest, and capable. Specifically, the total percentage value for Ambitious = 55.40, honest = 51.80, and capable = 44.70; N = 112.

Table 4.2

Top Three RVS Values for an Ideal Employee

RVS Value		Rank	Count	%
Ambitious		1	31	27.70
		2	19	17.00
		3	12	10.70
	Total			55.40
Honest		1	31	27.70
		2	17	15.20
		3	10	8.90
	Total			51.80
Capable		1	17	15.20
		2	20	17.90
		3	13	11.60
	Total			44.70
Note: N=112				

Research Question 2 Findings

Table 4.3 displays the differences between the bottom three ranked RVS values (out of 18 total values) for an "ideal employee." Bottom three ranks were defined as cumulative percentage by adding up frequency of responses for rank 18, 17, and 16 for a specified RVS value. Total percentage value was then calculated to determine rank order.

As indicated, leaders ranked the bottom three RVS values as loving, courageous, and obedient. Specifically, the total percentage value for loving (ranked #18) = 75.00, courageous (ranked # 17) = 39.10, and obedient (ranked # 16) = 17.90; N = 112.

Table 4.3

Bottom Three RVS Values For an Ideal Employee
Least Important for Ideal Employee

RVS Value		Rank	Count	%
Loving		18	57	50.90
		17	15	13.40
		16	12	10.70
	Total			75.00
Courageous		18	11	9.80
		17	14	12.50
		16	21	16.80
	Total			39.10
Obedient		18	8	7.10
		17	7	6.30
		16	5	4.50
	Total			17.90
Note: N=112				

Research Question 3 Findings

Table 4.4 displays the differences between the top three ranked RVS values leaders should possess in order to succeed in their business. Top three ranks were defined by cumulative percentage by adding up frequency of responses for rank 1, 2, and 3 for a specified RVS value. Total percentage value was then calculated to determine rank order. As indicated, leaders ranked the top three RVS values as Ambitious, honest, and responsible. Specifically, the total percentage value for Ambitious = 64.30, honest = 9.80, and capable = 43.80; N = 112.

Table 4.4

Top Three Most Important RVS Values Leaders Should Possess to Succeed Most Important for Success

RVS Value		Rank	Count	%
Ambitious		1	40	35.70
		2	16	14.30
		3	16	14.30
	Total			64.30
Honest		1	23	20.50
		2	12	10.70
		3	11	9.80
	Total			41.00
Responsible		1	17	15.20
		2	15	13.40
		3	17	15.20
	Total			43.80
Note: N=112				

Research Question 4 Findings

Table 4.5 displays the differences between the bottom three ranked RVS values leaders should possess in order to succeed in their business. Bottom three ranks were defined as cumulative percentage by adding up frequency of responses for rank 18, 17, and 16 for a specified RVS value. Total percentage value was then calculated to determine rank order. As indicated, leaders ranked the bottom three RVS values as loving obedient, and clean. Specifically, the total percentage value for loving = 81.20, honest = 9.80, and capable = 43.80; N = 112.

Table 4.5

Top Three Least Important RVS Values Leaders Should Possess to Succeed
Least Important for Success

RVS Value		Rank	Count	%
Loving		18	53	47.30
		17	24	21.40
		16	14	12.50
	Total			81.20
Obedient		18	18	16.10
		17	19	17.00
		16	12	10.70
	Total			43.80
Clean		18	11	9.80
		15	14	13.40
		16	9	8.00
	Total			31.20
Note: N=112				

Research Question 5 Findings

Table 4.6 displays the differences between age as clustered generationally and how they view the top three most important RVS values for an "ideal employee". As indicated, Gen X and Gen Y placed ambitious at the top of their list while Boomers ranked it second. Boomers ranked honest as number one where Gen X and Gen Y placed it third. Boomers picked capable as third. Gen Y ranked responsible as second and Gen X placed capable as second. While this focus was strictly on the most important values for an ideal employee, data does show potential diversity by generation.

Table 4.6

Generation by Top Three Most Important RVS Values For an Ideal Employee

| | Most Important for Success | | | | | | | | | | | |
| | Generation Y | | | | Generation X | | | | Generation Boomers | | | |
RVS Value	RVS Value	Rank	Count	%	RVS Value	Rank	Count	%	RVS Value	Rank	Count	%
Ambitious	Ambitious	1	10	35.70	Ambitious	1	11	25.60	Honest	1	13	31.70
		2	4	14.30		2	8	18.60		2	8	19.50
		3	3	10.70		3	1	2.30		3	5	12.20
				60.70				46.50				63.40
Responsible	Capable	1	17	15.20	Capable	1	9	20.90	Ambitious	1	10	24.40
		2	15	13.40		2	7	16.30		2	7	17.10
		3	17	15.20		3	5	11.60		3	8	19.50
				43.80				48.80				61.00
Honest	Honest	1	1	3.60	Honest	1	9	20.90	Capable	1	7	17.10
		2	6	21.40		2	6	14.00		2	7	17.10
		3	4	14.30		3	3	7.00		3	4	9.80
				39.30				41.90				44.00

Research Question 6 Findings

Table 4.7 displays the differences between the gender and top three most important RVS values for an "ideal employee". As indicated, Female leaders ranked responsible, honest, and Ambitious as the top three values most important for ideal follower while Male leaders ranked RVS values as Ambitious, honest, and capable.

Table 4.7
Gender by Top Three Most Important RVS Values For an Ideal Employee
Most Important for Success

	Female				Male	
RVS Value	**Rank**	**Count**	**%**	**RVS Value**	**Rank**	**Count**	**%**
Responsible	1	7	16.70	Ambitious	1	21	30.90
	2	9	21.40		2	13	19.10
	3	10	23.80		3	8	11.80
			61.90				61.80
Honest	1	10	23.80	Honest	1	21	30.90
	2	10	23.80		2	7	10.30
	3	1	2.40		3	9	13.20
			50.00				54.40
Ambitious	1	10	23.80	Capable	1	10	14.70
	2	6	14.30		2	14	20.60
	3	4	9.50		3	8	11.80
			47.60				47.10
Note: N=112							

Research Question 7 Findings

Table 4.8 displays the differences between the top three ranked industries and top three most important RVS values for an "ideal employee". As indicated, Retail ranked responsible, honest, and capable; Health Care chose responsible, honest, and Ambitious; and Accommodations picked responsible, ambitious, and honest.

Observations and Analysis of Survey Data

The Tri-States LMX Survey 2012 generated raw data from 112 completed cases, which enabled a two-fold analysis of RQ1 through RQ4. Initially, descriptive statistics were used to achieve a holistic overview of what the data were telling us and parametric and non-parametric tests were used to further evaluate the research questions. There were some interesting challenges identified by the data. For each of the 18 values in Scenario One and Scenario Two, calculated mean averages were straight forward, but a review of median averages indicated some issues, such as the top three values for Scenario One producing the same median average. It was decided that this would not be used due to the sample size being too small. Another reality stemmed from the nature of the survey design itself, since North Florida and Tri-States both required a mandatory rank order of all 18 values and no two items could share the same score. Theoretically, all 18 items with a shared ranking would illustrate the ultimate null hypothesis, which was impossible under this protocol. Another observation was the fact that there were no continuous variables, thus the use of Spearman Rho was not applicable, which is consistent with the findings of earlier researchers (Arsham, 2011; McDonald 2009; Braithwaite, 1994; Gibbins & Walker, 1993).

Scenario One (SC1) posed the first two research questions. RQ1 indicated leader preference of those values and associated behaviors deemed most important for ideal followers to possess, as evidenced by the top three rankings of ambitious, honest, and capable. RQ2 focused on the opposite end of the ranking scale identifying the least important traits for ideal followers, listing the bottom three as loving, courageous and obedient. Together these findings show support for H1a and H2a, which are interpreted together to show a difference in most and least desirable values and associated behaviors of followers. Tri-States RQ1 and RQ2 correspond to RQ1 in North Florida (Deckert, 2007).

Table 4.8

Most Important for Success

	Retail				Health Care				Accommodations			
RVS Value	Rank	Count	%	RVS Value	Rank	Count	%	RVS Value	Rank	Count	%
Responsible	1	4	16.70	Responsible	1	1	8.30	Responsible	1	2	15.40
	2	4	16.70		2	6	50.00		2	4	30.80
	3	6	25.00		3	2	16.70		3	3	23.10
			58.40				75.00				69.30
Honest	1	7	29.20	Honest	1	4	33.30	Ambitious	1	5	38.50
	2	2	8.30		2	4	33.30		2	2	15.40
	3	4	16.70		3	0	0.00		3	1	7.70
			54.20				66.60				61.60
Capable	1	3	12.50	Ambitious	1	3	25.00	Honest	1	3	23.10
	2	6	25.00		2	3	25.00		2	2	15.40
	3	4	16.70		3	1	8.30		3	1	7.70
			54.20				58.30				46.20

Top Three Ranked Industries by Top Three Most Important RVS Values For an Ideal Employee

Further support for H1a and H2a comes from parametric and non-parametric analyses applied to summaries of SC1 data. In order to create testable variables, data were averaged to give an overall mean score and a median score for each of the 18 values. An independent-samples t-test was conducted in order to examine the differences between mean rankings of most and least desirable characteristics of followers. The analysis revealed that the three most desirable follower traits (Responsible, Ambitious, and Honest) were ranked as significantly better (M = 4.566) than the three least desirable traits (Courageous, Forgiving, and Loving), M = 14.137, t(4) = 10.701, p < .001. The non-parametric Mann-Whitney U test on the medians echoes this significant result, z = - 2.087, p = .037. The average rank for most desirable traits was 2, while the average rank for least desirable traits was 5.

Scenario Two (SC2) applied the same RVS values list but challenged leaders to think in the context of their personal leadership role. RQ3 indicated leaders' top three choices as ambitious, honest, and responsible, for the most important values that make them successful leaders. RQ4 revealed the bottom three as obedient, loving and clean, for the least important values that make leaders successful. Together these findings show support for H3a and H4a, which are interpreted together to show a difference in most and least desirable values and associated behaviors of leaders. Tri-States RQ3 and RQ4 correspond to RQ2 in North Florida (Deckert, 2007).

A similar analysis to that applied for RQ1 and RQ2 was used to further assess RQ3 and RQ4. That is, it tested whether the three values ranked as most desirable and the three values ranked as least desirable for leaders differed significantly. For SC2, the three most desirable leader traits (Ambitious, Responsible, and Honest) were also ranked as significantly better (M = 4.759) than the three least desirable traits (Clean, Obedient, and Loving), M = 14.164, t(4) = 7.620, p = .002. The non-parametric Mann-Whitney U test on the medians is marginally significant, z = -1.964, p = .050. The average rank for most desirable traits was 2, while the average rank for least desirable traits was 5.

An additional independent-samples t-test was conducted in order to examine the differences between mean rankings of most and least desirable characteristics of followers and leaders. The mean ranking for top three most desirable traits for followers (M = 4.566, SD = .072) did not differ significantly from the mean ranking for leaders (M = 4.759, SD = .941), t(4) = .355, p = .741. The mean ranking for the three least desirable traits for followers (M = 14.137, SD = 1.548) also did not differ significantly from the mean ranking for leaders (M = 14.164, SD = 1.919).

The next three research questions went beyond the scope of the original North Florida (Deckert, 2007) study and were more difficult to evaluate. RQ5 introduced the variable of Age and corresponding data was grouped according to generational segments.

It is interesting to note that Boomers valued honest, ambitious, and capable for their top three, and Generation X chose ambitious, capable, and honest, showing a close value system between those two generations. On the other end of the age spectrum, Generation Y selected ambitious, responsible, and honest. While two items on their list match the two older generations, they do introduce the value of responsible in the top three.

Generational differences were also tested using mean rankings to determine if any difference existed in average mean rankings between specified independent variable. As the research questions were primarily interested in most desirable traits for these independent variables, least desirable traits were left out of the analyses. An analysis of variance was conducted to test for generational differences.

SPSS 20.0 Analyze/General Linear Model/Univariate (ANOVA) was used to test if there was a significant difference in the ranking of the three most desirable traits as ranked by the total sample (Ambitious, Responsible, and Honest) between generations.

Assumptions of normality and homogeneity of variance were not assessed due to small sample size. Results from the ANOVA test indicated that there was no difference between generations; $F(2, 6) = 1.009$, $p = .419$ (two-tailed). Boomers ranked the traits as 4.236 on average (SD = .286), Gen X ranked the traits as 4.488 on average (SD =.846), and Gen Y ranked the traits as 5.167 on average (SD = 1.127). Table 4.X displays a model summary of the ANOVA analysis for generational differences.

Table 4.9

Model Summary Generated from Multiple Regression Analysis of Generational Differences

Source Squares	Type III Sum of Squares	Mean	Partial Squared	Observed Power			
	1.390	2	0.695	1.009	0.419	0.252	0.155
Intercept	192.955	1	192.955	279.908	<.001	0.979	1.000
Generation	1.390	2	0.695	1.009	0.419	0.252	2.017
Error	4.136	6	0.689				
Total	198.481	9					
Corrected Total	5.527	8					

An additional non-parametric analysis confirmed non-significance. A Kruskal-Wallis test on the medians showed no significant difference among the three generational groups, .2(2) = 1.199, $p = .549$. The mean rank for Baby Boomers was 3.67, the mean rank for Generation X was 5.50, and the mean rank for Generation Y was 5.83.

RQ6 examined Gender, with women ranking the top three values as responsible, honest, and ambitious, which matches the same top three as Generation Y. Men chose ambitious, honest and capable for their top three, which matches the top picks by Boomers and Generation X.

Gender differences were also tested using mean rankings to determine if any difference existed in average mean rankings between specified independent variables, with the emphasis on the most desirable traits and least desirable traits were left out of the analyses. SPSS 20.0 Analyze/Compare Means/Independent Samples t-Test was used to test if there was a significant difference in the ranking of the three most desirable traits as ranked by the total sample (Ambitious, Responsible, and Honest) between genders. Results from the test indicated that there was no difference in ranking between males and females; $t(4) = 1.016$ $p = .367$ (two-tailed). Females ranked the traits as 4.746 on average (SD = 0.655) while males ranked the traits as 4.294 on average (SD = 0.406).

An additional non-parametric analysis confirmed non-significance. A Mann- Whitney U test on the medians showed no significant difference in ranking between men and women, $z = -1.091$, $p = .275$. The average rank for women was 4.33, while the average rank for men was 2.67.

RQ7 focused on 20 NAICS industry segments and posed the greatest difficulty for meaningful analysis. While 112 total cases is significant, distribution across 20 NAICS segments left at eight of them with five or fewer responses. As a result, analysis focused on the top three industry segments and their corresponding top three RVS values. Retail

Trade picked responsible, honest, and capable. Health Care & Social Assistance chose responsible, honest, and ambitious. Accommodations & Food Service selected responsible, ambitious, and honest.

SPSS 20.0 Analyze/General Linear Model/Univariate (ANOVA) was also used to test if there was a significant difference in the ranking of the three most desirable traits as ranked by the total sample (Ambitious, Responsible, and Honest) between individuals from the top three most common industries among survey respondents. Assumptions of normality and homogeneity of variance were not assessed due to small sample size. Results from the ANOVA test indicated that there was no difference between industries; $F(2, 6) = 2.167$, $p = .196$ (two-tailed). Individuals working in the retail industry ranked the traits as 4.792 on average (SD = .397), individuals working in health care ranked the traits as 3.722 on average (SD = .855), and individuals working in accommodations ranked the traits as 4.256 on average (SD = .546). Table 4.10 displays a model summary of the ANOVA analysis for industrial differences.

Table 4.10

Model Summary Generated from Multiple Regression Analysis of Industrial Differences

Source Squares	Type III Sum of Squares		Mean Squared			Partial Squared	Observed Power
Corrected Model	1.7.16*	2	0.858	2.167	0.196	0.419	0.287
Intercept	163.081	1	163.081	412.063	<.001	0.986	1.000
Industry	1.716	2	0.858	2.167	0.196	0.419	0.287
Error	2.375	6	0.396				
Total	167.171	9					
Corrected Total	4.090	8					

Note * R Squared = .419 (Adjusted R Squared = .226) b. Computed using alpha = .05

An additional non-parametric analysis confirmed non-significance. A Kruskal-Wallis test on the medians showed no significant difference among the most prevalent industries, .2(2) = 1.369, p = .504. The mean rank for the retail sector was 6.17, the mean rank for health care was 3.67, and the mean rank for accommodations was 5.17. Chapter Five expands on these thoughts and provide recommendations for future consideration and research.

CHAPTER FIVE: DISCUSSIONS, CONCLUSIONS & RECOMMENDATIONS

Discussion of Findings

Followership in the Tri-States: values and behaviors deemed most desirable by small business leaders, is a scholarly research study seeking to share a comprehensive overview of the science of management theory. Evolving LMX theory is at the forefront of this evolutionary journey and demonstrated by the value of studies like the Tri-States LMX Survey 2012. This was affirmed by a variety of small business leaders when they reflected on leadership and noted if they turn around and no one is following them, they knew it was going to be a rough day. Although causal relationships were not examined in this study, such a commonly shared concern and fear may have been a compelling motivation for participants and validates the need for on-going research of leader-follower relationships in small businesses.

Chapter One Synopsis

Chapter One provided an overview as to the science of management theory over thousands of years as critiqued by a diverse audience of noteworthy scholars (Kelley, 1988; Beckerleg, 2002; Johnson, 2003; Rosenau, 2004; Stewart, 2003). The emerging phenomenon of LMX (Danserau, Graen & Haga, 1975) and HQDR (Erdogan, Kraimer, & Liden, 2004) are natural extensions of evolving research questioning the value of followership, capped by the Deckert (2007) study of Followership in North Florida, redirecting research analysis away from large corporate settings to small business instead, a critical engine driving the U.S. Economy (Drabenstott, 2008). Along the way, several key ideas were discussed: followers out-number leaders; studies of followership are only just emerging; and historically, management education emphasizes trait-templates as opposed to process (Lundin & Lancaster, 1990; Wren, 1995; and Rusher, 2005).

This study promised two items of significance: 1) that leaders and followers of participating companies could better understand each other's role in a HQDR; and 2) that other third party non-participants would also benefit by gaining knowledge that may contribute to improving their organizational effectiveness. Tri-States responded to Deckert's (2007) call for further research and provides a baseline for a comparison to North Florida, while examining the potential influence age, gender and industry, three new areas of understanding.

Chapter Two Synopsis

Chapter Two documents a solid theoretical basis for this study and suggests key connections across a diverse range of topics. Complexity economics prescribes economic development and the creation of wealth as highly adaptive, evolutionary cycles grounded in a very human process of choice, chance and change, subject to flawed decisions along the way (Beinhocker, 2007). This is characteristic of a leader's choice of followers to hire and an employee's choice of leaders to follow. Small business leaders as entrepreneurs identify and satisfy people's needs, wants and desires, undertaking a journey fraught with risk and dependent on innovation and information to thrive and survive (Gartner, 1985; Drucker, 1985; Sobel, 2006; Ennis, 2008; Beinhocker, 2007).

Information on why people follow is vital to this process. Historically, leadership has been prescribed as a list of traits (Bass. 1990a) and competencies (Katz & Kahn, 1978) which are extremely fluid and flow across several organizational layers (Sharma, 1997).

Followership recognizes that there are no leaders without followers (Collinson, 2001), leaders are dependent upon creative collaboration with followers (Bennis, 2009), and the dynamics of effective followership are value-driven (Meilinger, 1994; Solovy, 2005; & Kelley, 1992).

LMX theory outlines a relationship process (Dansereau, et al., 1975) in which leaders sort followers into in-groups and out-groups (Graen & Uhl-Bien, 1995), forming a complex HQDR where the relationship is as vital as the functional attributes (Dienisch & Liden, 1986). One aspect of this relationship is called value-behavior relationship

(Katz & Kahn, 1978) and prescribes how followers who understand their work environment and which values leaders expect, increase the likelihood of transitioning to an in-group, ultimately benefiting the leader and organization (Sparrowe & Liden, 1997).

Defining values is grounded on seminal research by Rokeach (1978) which demonstrated that values shape each person's actions, attitudes, and choices – terminal values represent end-states and instrumental values signify moral or competency values, the latter of which populate job descriptions (O'Reilly, 1991). Values are essential determinants in shaping one's behavior in a system known as value-behavior dynamic (England, 1967; Blood, 1969; England & Lee, 1974; Feather, 1995). Understanding this dynamic provides a linkage to grasping team performance, once elements of power and cooperation are identified (Chatman & Barsade, 1995). Ultimately, when two people think alike or share cognitive functioning, they tend to share values, use a common communications systems, interpret and process information similarly (Meglino et al., 1989; Rokeach, 1973) embodying the complex relationship between LMX and values. Value congruence is measurable (Gilbert, 1985), sustains HQDR (Erdogan, 2004), and leads to better collaboration, job satisfaction, and organizational commitment (Schein, 19875; Deckert, 20070.

LMX and its related attributes, help decipher how small business entrepreneurs: are motivated (Wiklund, 2003), define success (Stavrou et al., 2005), apply operational control on the internal workforce (Drucker, 2004), the differentiation of labor (Kotey & Slade, 2005; Blau, 1970), and the context in which competitive intelligence is processed

(Haugh & McKee, 2004). Ultimately, leader values have been linked to internal and external traits behind organizational effectiveness (Rogoff, Lee, & Suh, 2004) and lists of preferred leadership traits (Posner & Schmidt, 1992; Kotey & Meredith, 1997). While most research is centered on large corporations (Heneman, Tansky, & Camp, 2000;

Hornsby & Kuratko,. 2003), the emergence of studies like North Florida (Deckert, 2007) and this study, directly respond to the call for further researched focused on the small business enterprise (Purcell, 1993).

The future benefit to small business leaders who use LMX research to improve organizational effectiveness will be measurable and enhanced by an increased understanding of those values local business leaders deem most important for followers to model. This will lead to the evolution of a leader's ideal follower model and add to the overall body of LMX knowledge for followers, leaders, and organizations alike.

Chapter Three Synopsis

Chapter Three defined statistical tools (Reswick, 1994; Inu, 1991; Simon & Francis, 2001) and quantitative research methodology appropriate for applying the Rokeach Values survey [RVS] (1973) adapted by Deckert (2007) rank ordering 18 instrumental values and associated behaviors. Small business leaders would be asked to determine the top three most important and bottom three least important values ideal followers should possess. Leaders would also be asked to list the top three most important and the bottom three least important values for their personal success as a leader. RVS integrity is widely acclaimed (Payne, 1988; Braithwaite, 1994; Agle,

Mitchell, & Sonnenfeld, 1999; McDonald, 2009) and provides a solicitation process that was simple, non-threatening, and straightforward (Fischoff, 1991; Cresswell, 2009). Seven research questions are identified, each with an alternate hypothesis and null hypothesis.

Across the Tri-States, 1,279 Stage 2 & Stage 3 business were culled from 15,639 total businesses. Two hundred and seventy seven public sector employees were omitted reducing the sample population to 1,002. A target sample size of 278 was calculated (Raosoft®, 2011), with a second tier of 200 additional targets identified to insure the goal of 66-183 cases would be met in order to achieve statistical significance (Tabachnick & Fidell, 2007). Simple random sampling techniques were followed (Cooper & Schindler, 2008).

Participants provided demographic information for educational level, years of small business leadership experience, age, gender, and industry. Respondents also rank ordered the same instrumental values list for each of two scenarios. Causal relationships behind leader choices were not part of the study and the top three and bottom three rankings overall were emphasized.

Chapter Four Synopsis

Chapter Four opened with a summary of the linkage between the science of management with its historical emphasis on leadership traits (Lundin & Lancaster, 1990) and contemporary research centered on leader-follower exchange [LMX] (Dixon & Westbrook, 2003). Tri-States embraced the premise that human behavior is driven by values and associated behaviors (Rokeach, (1973), and applied two scenarios based on a

RVS list of 18 instrumental values and associated behaviors to 359 Stage 2 & Stage 2 small business leaders across the Tri-States. Descriptive statistics methods were applied to raw data collected from the Tri-States LMX Survey 2012, using SPSS for coding and tabulating. Means and median averages were computed and parametric and nonparametric testing were selectively applied as appropriate to the data. Sample size and the ordinal nature of the rank ordering process were complex challenges. The Tri-States LMX Survey 2012 direct solicitation generated a significant response rate of 32.9 percent and 112 completed surveys, and a demographic profile representing the target sample was provided.

Data for each of the seven research questions is documented. RQ1 found leaders deemed follower RVS values of ambitious, honest, and capable (see Table 4.2) as the most important, while RQ2 identified leader preferences for least important to be obedient, courageous, and loving (see Table 4.3). This, along with additional parametric and non-parametric analyses, provides support for H1a and H2a .

H3a and H4a were supported by the fact that RQ3 listed most important leader preferences for leadership roles as ambitious, honest and responsible (see Table 4.4), while RQ4 showed leader preference for least important as clean, obedient, and loving (see Table 4.5). Additional support for H3a and H4a comes from both parametric and non-parametric analyses as provided in Chapter 4.

RQ5 examined whether generational age groups displayed differences in RVS values considered most important for followers. Baby Boomers and Generation X both rated honest, ambitious, and capable as the top three most valued behaviors, albeit in slightly different orders. Generation Y also chose ambitions and honest as two of the most valued behaviors, but selected responsible as a third. While there appears to be some difference in the values ranked as top three as evident from the descriptive analysis, no statistically significant difference in the overall top three ranked traits was found between generational status. This is likely due to the inappropriately small sample size used in the parametric and non-parametric analysis. While the parametric analysis does not support H5a , the descriptive information showing differences in top three choices provides some anecdotal support for the alternative hypothesis.

RQ6 examined whether the different genders displayed differences in RVS values considered most important for followers. Women ranked the top three values as responsible, honest, and

ambitions, while men ranked the top three as ambitious, honest, and capable. While there is no statistical difference in how men and women ranked the top three overall preferred behaviors and therefore no statistical support for H6a , this is likely due to the inappropriately small sample size used for the parametric analysis.

Despite the lack of statistical support, information from the descriptive discussion provides some anecdotal support for H6a .

RQ7 examined the effect of industry on ranking of the top three values for followers, specifically for differences among the top three industries represented in the sample. Individuals working in Retail Trade chose responsible, honest, and capable, while individuals in Health Care & Social Assistance and Accommodations & Food

Service both chose responsible, honest, and ambitious, albeit in slightly different orders.

Once again, no statistical support was gained for the alternative hypothesis from the parametric analysis. Although there was no statistical difference in the rankings of the three characteristics considered most desirable by the entire respondent pool, the diversity of top three ranked choices evident from the descriptive discussion shows some anecdotal support for H7a .

The role of value congruence and HQDR as they contribute to organizational effectiveness was upheld. As a result, a working model for ideal followers and successful leaders in the Tri-State small business market was provided.

Conclusions

A major objective for this research study was to achieve such a level of statistical significance, that a meaningful comparison analysis between Tri-States LMX Survey 2012 and the Foundations of Followership study in North Florida (Deckert, 2007) would be produced. This study met that challenge, responded to Deckert's call for further research in new geographical areas, and provided a new step in LMX research pertaining to small business. In that context, a specific purpose behind this study was the documentation and analysis of those values and associated behaviors small business leaders' deemed most and least important for followers to possess as ideal followers, and that contributed to their success as a leader.

Logistic Comparisons - North Florida versus Tri-States

Tri-States used North Florida's (Deckert, 2007) pioneering effort as a source of inspiration. In that context, it is important to note similarities between the two studies:

1.   Both used the Rokeach (1973) list of 18 RVS Instrumental Values, and as adapted for North Florida,

2. Education and years of leadership experience were measured,

3. Both targeted small business leaders,

4. Each utilized a unique access code,

5. RQ1 in North Florida became RQ1 & RQ2 in Tri-States, and RQ2 in North Florida became RQ3 & RQ4 in Tri-States,

6. Both took approximately three weeks in field research data collection,

7. Both were administered online,

8. Both surveys focused on the top three most important and bottom three least important value rankings overall.

On the other hand, there are several differences between North Florida and Tri-States providing a noteworthy distinction between the two studies:

1. Tri-States adopted small business definitions provided by the Edward Lowe Foundation (2011), emphasizing Stage 2 (10-99 employees) & Stage 3 (100- 499 employees) private companies, excluding public sector employers. In contrast, Deckert (2007) used the U.S. Small Business Administration's Central Contractor Registry (CCR), database, targeting companies of 559 or fewer employees with a main operation in North Florida. While North Florida's sample population were only CCR companies, Tri-States sample population included all private companies, some of which were also a government contractor but that clarification was not asked or necessary;

2. North Florida filtered down from 423,430 CCR companies to a sample population of 1,339 with a targeted sample of 500 with a goal of 25-50 completions. Tri-States started with 15,639 total companies which filtered down to 1,002 Stage 2 & 3 companies with a target sample of 278 plus up to 200 more if needed to achieve statistical significance to achieve a goal of 66 to 183 completions,

3. North Florida achieved 29 completed cases versus 112 in the Tri-States,

4. North Florida is an urban setting with high population density in contrast to Tri-States which is rural with low population density,

5. North Florida targeted government contractors capping employee size at 559 or less, while Tri-States targeted all Stage 2 & 3 private employers with 10 to 499 employees,

6. Tri-States introduced three new dimensions for discussion:

a. age through analysis of generational cluster (RQ5),

b. gender (RQ6) and,

c. industry (RQ7) taking the top three segments of retail trade, health care & social assistance, and accommodations & food services,

Findings – North Florida versus Tri-States

It is imperative that a comparison also be made of the findings realized in North Florida in contrast to the findings generated by Tri-States. Deckert's call for future research specifically suggested a benefit of reviewing how findings from future studies might compare to North Florida as a benchmark.

Table 5.1 below, summarizes a simple comparison of the top three and bottom three rankings by leaders in North Florida in contrast to leaders in Tri-States. North Florida's RQ1 had a part A and part B, which corresponds to Tri-State's RQ1 and RQ2 respectively. North Florida's RQ2 also had a part A and part B that correspond to Tri- State's RQ3 and RQ4 respectively.

Table 5.1

RVS Rankings: North Florida vs. Tri-States Top and Bottom Three Ranked Values
Top Three Most Important

	North Florida	Tri-States	
RQ1a	Responsible*#+	Ambitious*#+	RQ1
	Capable*#+	Honest*#+	
	Honest*#+	Capable*#+	
	Honest	Ambitious	
RQ2a	Responsible	Honest	RQ3
	Capable	Responsible	
Bottom Three Least Important			
	North Florida	Tri-States	
RQ1b	Forgiving	Obedient	RQ2
	Clean	Courageous	
	Loving	Loving	
	Obedient	Clean	
RQ2b	Clean	Obedient	RQ4
	Loving	Loving	

NOTE: Tri-States data came from this research study, North Florida data came from Deckert, 2007.

As depicted in Table 5.1 above, North Florida's ranking of top three follower values listed responsible as number one while Tri-States listed ambitious instead. Both recognize capable and honest. In top three leader traits, North Florida ranked capable as number one while Tri-States ranked ambitious. Both recognized honest and responsible.

In bottom three follower traits, North Florida listed forgiving and clean, while Tri-States listed obedient and courageous. Both listed loving in 18th place as the least important Tri-States North Florida value. As for the bottom three leader values, although the order differed, both ranked obedient and clean, while both placed loving in 18th place as least important.

North Florida did not provide any data relevant to RQ5, RQ6 and RQ7 from the Tri-States study, which is summarized extensively in Tables 4.6, 4.7, and 4.8 in Chapter Four, depicting all values listed for RQ1a and RQ1 in Table 5.1 above, * for generational age, # for gender, and + for top three industries.

Table 5.2 below, compares North Florida to Tri-States for education and years of leadership experience. The largest percentage distribution for education was 34.5 percent for a Master's Degree in North Florida versus 40.2 percent with a Bachelor's degree in Tri- States. In years of leadership experience, in North Florida 34.5 percent held 16+ years versus a tie in Tri-States at 21.4 percent, with one to five years and 16+ years. Two observations worth noting: 1) no leaders in North Florida were in the No HSD category while .9 percent in Tri-States were and, 2) no leaders in North Florida had less than one year experience while in Tri-States 10.6 percent were new in their roles.

Table 5.2

Education & Experience: North Florida vs. Tri-States Percentage Distribution

Education

North Florida	0	No HSD	9	Tri-States
	27.5	HSD	24.1	
	-	AA	40.2	
	24.1	BA/BS	9.8	
	34.5	MA/MS/MBA	12.5	
	13.8	PHD/JD/DBA		

Years of Leadership Experience

North Florida	0	<1	10.6	Tri-States
	31.0	1-5	21.4	
	10.3	6-10	19.5	
	24.2	11-15	14.1	
	34.5	16+	21.4	

Note: Tri-States data came from this research study, North Florida came from Deckert, 2007

As a reminder, this study does not offer any analysis of causal relationships behind results. North Florida is urban-based and used private small businesses that were government contractors. Tri-States broadly focused on private small businesses in a rural area. This analysis documents a noteworthy comparison of the two research studies but does not provide any causal analysis behind the data.

Implications for Practice

Chapter one of this study stated two items of significance. First, the expectation that leaders and followers could better understand each other's role in a HQDR. Participating leaders and their designation of ambitious, honest and capable as the three most important preferred values for an ideal follower evidence this. Ambitious implies an expectation of not being satisfied with the status quo and wanting more. Honest implies a sense of trust and in a small business where everyone wears several hats, a team like a chain, is only as strong as its weakest link, and honesty is a core value. Capable is meeting and exceeding expectations in a reliable and dependable way, getting the job done.

Likewise, when the same leaders listed those values most important to their success, it is interesting they flagged ambitious, honest, and responsible. The first two demonstrate a compatible expectation for followers and leaders alike, while responsible, conveys a mature understanding that the buck stops with them as the leader. During Tri-State's direct solicitation many of the selected leaders offered the observation that this exercise would give them the opportunity to define their feelings or ideas, but in a tangible way. This is commendable since quality information is strategic to sustaining and cultivating a HQDR.

This understanding leads to value congruence, that point at which leaders and followers can share the same understanding as to which values leaders deem most important for follower success, and how those same values parallel the most important behaviors for leader success. Value congruence leads to increased job effectiveness and satisfaction, and the likelihood of achieving a HQDR.

A second item of significance is the value added benefit of knowledge cultivated from this analysis and its immediate benefit to other small business leaders across the area. The diversity of gender, age and industry reinforced the universal appeal of survey results and its potential application generically to other small Stage 2 & 3 Tri-State businesses. The marketplace is extremely competitive, so it behooves every employer in the race to recruit quality team members from the same limited supply of talent in small rural areas, to be tuned into those values and attributes most important for achieving a HQDR. Those environments that achieve it can expect improved employee morale, retention, and productivity.

A side note to this moment of reflection, is the fact that every data segment tagged in the Tri-States survey: leader, follower, age by generation, gender, and two of the three top industries, picked ambitious as one the top three most important values (see Table 4.8). The only data segment that did not list ambitious is the industry retail group, which listed capable instead, which the other two industries omitted from their top three. While this study did not examine causal relationships, this does beg the question, is ambitious a reflection of the stereotype for Midwestern work ethic? It also raises the question, did retailers emphasize capable because their very business nature is totally profit focused?

Possible questions for future researchers to explore.

Recommendations for Further Research

Deckert's (2007) original challenge for further research in additional geographic locations continues to be a sound idea. The evolution of newer research will expand requisite knowledge about LMX theory as it influences small business and create a more accurate holistic overview of the topic nationally. In addition, the possible adaptation of the North Florida RVS tool in other global settings would allow future researchers to make comparisons of multi-cultural diversity on a global stage. This researcher recommends using the Stage 2 & 3 criteria (Edward Lowe Foundation, 2011) in the U.S., whereas globally, comparable data regarding company size of 10 to 499 employees is not readily available. Such a universal global standard would be beneficial to expanding small business research efforts such as this study.

An interesting follow up study for future research, would be revisiting the same participating companies in North Florida and Tri-States, and administer the same survey tool to their employees, adapted for the follower's perspective, ranking leaders and then identifying those traits they deem most important to follower success. It would provide an interesting comparison to the original research to see how closely leaders and followers see things and significantly advance a broader perspective to LMX theory across both sides of the relationship.

This study also demonstrates that age by generational cluster, gender, and industry; do influence value-ranking preference. Future research may help understand that dynamic and what the causal attributes might be. For example, did boomers pick honesty as the number one trait because they are more cynical and sensitive to politics and unfulfilled promises in the workplace? Whereas generation X and Y see ambition as the key to career promotion and success?

The strong correlation between healthy HQDR relationships, value congruence, and organizational effectiveness was noted in several LMX studies and was substantiated in this study. Leaders do have preferences and other demographic variables do influence those choices. A topic that remains open for future study is the possible linkage of RVS values to psychometric profiling to see if preferred values explicit to a specific employment setting can be incorporated in a selection tool so hiring, screening, and staff development activities can reflect a HQDR orientation, in a truly customized fashion tailored to age, gender and industry explicitly?

Challenges associated with statistical analysis associated with this survey and the complexity of producing meaningful data associated with median scores and the nature of the ordinal rank order design of the survey instrument, are consistent with observations of earlier researchers (Arsham, 2011; McDonald, 2009; Braithwaite, 1994; Braithwaite & Law, 1985; and Ray, 1970). Caution must be exercised in avoiding the presumption that traditional statistical methods should be the analytical tool of choice when descriptive statistical methods still allow for reaching meaningful conclusions in the absence of continuous variables or datasets large enough to provide meaningful conclusions. In that context, future research that remains open for an indefinite period of time, and incorporates a Likert-rating scale, might provide large datasets and continuous variables for improved quantitative analysis and study.

In Conclusion, this dissertation research study fulfilled its mission and defined the top three and bottom three small business leader preferences for RVS instrumental values for ideal followers and leaders. The Tri-States LMX Survey 2012 achieved significant statistical results and provided data analysis that added to the body of LMX knowledge, as it pertains to small business settings. Several new areas of potential future LMX research were identified. While this principle investigator could not have anticipated the ultimate destination, the journey has proven to be enlightening and fruitful. In today's global economy, increasing sensitivity to multicultural diversity and the strategic benefit of quality team relationships grounded in core values of mutual trust, are essential to achieving small business excellence.

Bennis and Nanus (2003) said it best, "Organizational learning is the process by which an organization obtains and uses new knowledge, tools, behaviors and values," (p. 178). Followership in the Tri-States provides a new opportunity in organizational learning agility by small business owners who clearly value ideal employees with core values that parallel their own, for the good of the enterprise. In this difficult economic time, anything that adds values to the small business segment that historically creates the largest number of new jobs in the U.S.A. is a very good thing.

REFERENCES

Acs, Z. J. (1992). Small business economics: A global perspective. *Challenge, 35*(6), 38. Retrieved from ABI/INFORM Global. (Document ID:273754).

Acs, Z. J., Braunerhjelm, P., Audretsch, D., & Carlsson, B. (2009). The knowledge spillover theory of entrepreneurship. *Small Business Economics, 32*(1), 15-30. Retrieved from ABI/INFORM Global. (Document ID:1617565091).

Ács, Z. J., &Varga, A. (2005). Entrepreneurship, agglomeration and technological change. *Small Business Economics, 24*(3), 323-334. Retrieved from ABI/INFORM Global. (Document ID:824393641).

Adkins, C. L., Russell, C. J., & Warble, J. D. (1994). Judgments of fit in the selection process: The role of work value congruence. *Personnel Psychology, 47*(3), 653-656.

Agle, B. R., Mitchell, R. K., & Sonnenfeld, J. A. (1999). Who matters most to CEOs? An investigation of stakeholder attributes and salience, corporate performance, and CEO values. *Academy of Management Journal, 42*(5), 507-525.

Allport, G. W., & Odbert, H. S. (1936). Trait-names: A psycho-lexical study. *Psychological Monographs, 47*, 211.

Anderson, N. H. (1968). Likableness ratings of 555 personality-trait words. *Journal of Personality and Social Psychology, 9*(3), 272-279.

Arikan, A. (2010). Regional entrepreneurial transformation: A complex systems perspective. *Journal of Small Business Management, 48*(2), 152-173. doi:10.1111/j.1540-627X.2010.00290.x

Arsham, H. (2011). Statistical data analysis: Prove it with data. Retrieved from http://ubmail.ubalt.edu/~harsham/stat-data/opre330.htm

Ashkanasy, N. M., & O'Connor, C. (1997). Value congruence in leader member exchange. *The Journal of Social Psychology, 137*(5), 647-662.

Atkinson, R. D., & Andes, S. (2008, November). The 2008 state new economy index: Benchmarking economic transformation in the states. Retrieved from http://www.kauffman.org

Banutu-Gomez, M. (2004).Great leaders teach exemplary followership and serve as servant leaders. *The Journal of American Academy of Business, 4*(1/2), 143-151.

Bass, B. M. (1985). Leadership: Good, better, best. *Organizational Dynamics, 13*(3), 26-40.

Bass, B. M. (1990a). *Bass & Stogdill's handbook of leadership: Theory, research, and managerial applications* (3rd ed.). New York, NY: Free Press.

Bass, B. M. (1990b). From transactional to transformational leadership: Learning to share the vision. *Organizational Dynamics, 18*(3), 19-31.

Becker, B. W., & Connor, P. E. (1981). Personal values of the heavy user of mass media. *Journal of Advertising Research, 21,* 37-43.

Becker, T. E., Billings, R. S., Eveleth, D. M., & Gilbert, N. L. (1996). Foci and bases of employee commitment: Implications for job performance. *Academy of Management Journal, 39*(2), 464-482.

Beckerleg, C. N. (2002). An exploration of the practice of followership by school principals. (Doctoral dissertation). Retrieved from Dissertations & Thesis Full Text Database. (ATT 304 7612)

Beinhocker, E. D. (2007). *The origin of wealth: The radical remaking of economics and what it means for business and society.* Boston, MA: Harvard Business School Press.

Bennis, W. (1988). Ten traits of dynamic leaders. *Executive Excellence, 5*(2), 8-10.

Bennis, W. (1991). Leading followers: Following leaders. *Executive Excellence, 8*(6), 5-8.

Bennis, W. (1996). Leader as transformer. *Executive Excellence, 13*(10), 15.

Bennis, W. (1999). *Managing people is like herding cats: Warren Bennis on leadership.* New York: Executive Excellence Publishing.

Bennis, W. (2005). Seven stages of leadership. *Leadership Excellence, 22*(2), 3.

Bennis, W. (2009). On becoming a leader: The leadership classic 20th anniversary edition. Philadelphia: Perseus Books.

Bergsjo, P. (1999). Qualitative and quantitative research - Is there a gap, or only verbal disagreement? *Acta Obstetricia et Gynecologica Scandinavica, 78,* 559-562.

Blau, P. M. (1972). Interdependence and hierarchy in organizations. *Social Science Research, 1*(1), 1-24.

Blood, M. R. (1969). Work values and job satisfaction. *Journal of Applied Psychology, 53*(6), 456- 459.

Boutelle, J. (2004, April). Understanding organizational stakeholders for design success. *Boxes and arrows,* November 2011. Retrieved from http://www.boxesandarrows.com/view/understanding_organizational_stakeholder s_for_design_success#comments

Braithwaite, V. A. (1994). Beyond Rokeach's equality-freedom model: Two dimensional values in a one dimensional world. *Journal of Social Issues, 50*(4), 67-94.

Braithwaite, V. A., & Law, H. G. (1985). Structure of human values: Testing the adequacy of the Rokeach value survey. *Journal of Personality and Social Psychology, 49*(1), 250-263.

Buelow, D. M., & Hess, R. (2010, July) *Be bold Wisconsin: The Wisconsin competitiveness study.* Chicago, IL: Deloitte Development.

Burns, J. M. (1978). *Leadership.* New York, NY: Harper & Row.

Burns, J. M. (2003). *Transforming leadership: A new pursuit of happiness.* New York, NY: Grove Press.

Cable, D. M., & Judge, T. A. (1997). Interviewers' perceptions of person-organization fit and organizational selection decisions. *Journal of Applied Psychology, 82*(4), 546-561.

Cable, D. M., & Parsons, C. K. (2001). Socialization tactics and person-organization fit. *Personnel Psychology, 54*(1), 1-23.

Callanan, G. (2004). What would Machiavelli think? An overview of the leadership challenges in team based structures. *Team Performance Management, 10*(3/4), 77-84.

Chatman, J., & Barsade, S. G. (1995). Personality, organizational culture, and cooperation: Evidence from a business simulation. *Administrative Science Quarterly, 40*(3), 423-443.

Chatman, J. (1989). Improving interactional organizational research: A model of person organization fit. *Academy of Management Review, 14*(3), 333-349.

Chell, E., & Tracey, P. (2005). Relationship building in small firms: The development of a model. *Human Relations, 58*(5), 577-616.

Colangelo, A. J. (2000). *Followership: Leadership styles.* (Unpublished doctoral dissertation). University of Oklahoma, Norman.

Collins, J. (2001). *Good to great: Why some companies make the leap–and others don't.* New York, NY: Harper Collins.

Collinson, D. (2006). Rethinking followership: A post-structuralist analysis of follower identities. *The Leadership Quarterly. 17*(2), 179-189. doi:10.1016/j.leaqua.2005.12.005

Cone, J. D., & Foster, S. L. (2006). *Dissertations and theses from start to finish: psychology and related fields.* (2nd ed.). Washington D.C.: American Psychological Association.

Cooper, D. R., & Shindler, P. S. (2003). *Business research methods* (8th ed.). New York, NY: McGraw-Hill Irwin.

Cooper, D. R., & Schindler, P. S. (2008). *Business research methods* (10th ed.). Boston, MA: McGraw-Hill Irwin.

Cordello, V. (2011, February 24). I see Bill Drayton as I see Mahatma Gandhi. Retrieved from http://www.ashoka.org/story/i-see-bill-drayton-i-see-mahatma-gandhi

Creative Commons Corporation. (2011). *Rokeach value survey.* Retrieved October 3, 2011, from: http://www.facebook.com/pages/Rokeach-Value-Survey/135671809797626

Creswell, J. W. (2009). *Research design: Qualitative, quantitative, and mixed methods approach* (3rd ed.). Los Angeles, CA: Sage.

Dalton, D. R., & Todor, W. D. (1979). Turnover turned over: an expanded and positive perspective. *Academy of Management Review, 4*(2), 225-235.

Dansereau, F., Graen, G. B., & Haga, W. J. (1975). A vertical dyad linkage approach to leadership in formal organizations. *Organizational Behavior and Human Performance, 13*(1), 46-78.

Davidson, P. (1989). Entrepreneurship—and after? A study of growth willingness in small firms. *Journal of Business Venturing, 4*(3), 211–226.

Deckert, T. J. (2007). *Foundations of followership: A study identifying the values and behaviors deemed most desirable by small business leaders in North Florida,*(Doctoral dissertation). Available from Proquest Dissertations & Theses database. (Publication No. AAT 3254716).

Delmar, F. (1996). *Entrepreneurial behavior and business performance.* (Unpublished doctoral dissertation). Stockholm School of Economics, Stockholm.

Delmar, F., & Shane, S. (2004). Legitimizing first: Organizing activities and the survival of new ventures. *Journal of Business Venturing, 19*(3), 385-410. doi:10.1.1.200.2493. Retrieved from http://faculty.weatherhead.case.edu/shane/fop/FOP3.pdf

Diener, E., Larsen, R., & Emmons, R. (1984). Person x situation interactions: Choice of situations and congruence response models. *Journal of Personality and Social Psychology, 47*(3), 580-592.

Dienesch, R., & Liden, R. (1986). Leader member exchange model of leadership: A critique and further development. *Academy of Management Review, 11*(3), 618-635.

Dixon, G., & Westbrook, J. (2003). Followers revealed. *Engineering Management Journal, 15*(1), 19-26.

Doman, D. (2011). Happy cows produce more milk and happy worker produce more everything. *Ezinearticles.com.* Retrieved from http://ezinearticles.com/?Happy-Cows-Produce-More-Milk-and-Happy-Workers-Produce-More-Everything&id=970320

Drabenstott, M. (2008). *A 21st century strategy for the Riverlands.* RUPRI Center for Regional Competiveness: University of Missouri-Columbia. Retrieved from http://www.rupri.org

Drabenstott, M., & Moore, S. (2009). *Rural America in deep downturn: A RUPRI rural economic update.* RUPRI Center for Regional Competitiveness. Kansas City, MO. Retrieved from www.rupri.org/regionalcomp.php

Drabenstott, M., & Moore, S. (2010). *Past silos and smokestacks: Transforming the rural economy in the Midwest. Heartland papers.* Chicago, IL: The Chicago Council on Global Affairs.

Drath, W. H., & Palus, C. J. (1994). *Making common sense: Leadership as meaning-making in a community of practice.* Greensboro, NC: CCL Press.

Drucker, P. (1985). *Innovation and entrepreneurship: Practice and principles.* New York, NY: Harper & Row.

Drucker, P. F. (2004, June). What makes an effective executive? *Harvard Business Review, 82*(6), 58-63, 136.

Duarte, N., Goodson, J., & Klich, N. (1994). Effects of dyadic quality and duration on performance appraisal. *Academy of Management, 37*(3), 499-521.

Duchon, D., Green, S., & Taber, T. (1986). Vertical dyad linkage: A longitudinal assessment of antecedents, measures, and consequences. *Journal of Applied Psychology, 71*(1), 56-60.

Edward Lowe Foundation. (2009). Retrieved from http://www.edwardlowe.org

Edward Lowe Foundation. (2010a). *Economic gardening: An entrepreneur-oriented approach to economic prosperity.* Retrieved from http://www.ceonexus.com/documents/ELF-EGstorypuzzleV1082809.pdf

Edward Lowe Foundation.(2010b). *Second-stage entrepreneurs: Characteristics of second-stage.* Retrieved from http://edwardlowe.org/index.elf?page=s

Edward Lowe Foundation. (2011). *YourEconomy.org.* Retrieved from Edward Lowe Foundation website: http://www.edwardlowe.org/whatWeDo/yourEconomy.elf

England, G. W. (1967). Organizational goals and expected behavior of American managers. *Academy of Management Journal, 10*(2), 107-117.

England, G. W., & Lee, R. (1974). The relationship between managerial values and managerial success in the United States, Japan, England, and Australia. *Journal of Applied Psychology, 59*(4), 411-419.

Engle, E. M., & Lord, R. G. (1997). Implicit theories, self-schemas, and leader member exchange. *Academy of Management Journal, 40*(4), 988-1010.

Ennis, M. R. (2008, January 29). Competency models: A review of the literature and the role of employment and training administration (ETA). *Division of Research and Evaluation, Office of Policy Development and Research, Employment and Training Administration, U.S. Department of Labor.* Retrieved March 24, 2010 from http://www.careeronestop.org/competencymodel/info_documents/ OPDRLiteratureReview.pdf

Enzenauer, R. W. (2004). Leadership insights of Xenophon. *Physician Executive, 30*(4), 34-37.

Erdogan, B., Kraimer, M. L., & Liden, R. C. (2004). Work value congruence and intrinsic career success: The compensatory roles of leader member exchange and perceived organizational support. *Personnel Psychology, 57*(2), 305-332.

Fagiano, D. (1997). Managers vs. leaders: A corporate fable. *Management Review, 86*(10), 5-6.

Feather, N. T. (1995). Values, valences, and choice: The influence of values on the perceived attractiveness and choice of alternatives. *Journal of Personality and Psychology, 68*(6), 1135-1151.

Feather, N. T., & Peay, E. R. (1975). The structure of terminal and instrumental values: dimensions and clusters. *Australian Journal of Psychology, 27*(2), 151-164.

Fernandez, J. E., & Hogan, R. T. (2002). Values-based leadership. *The Journal for Quality and Participation, 25*(4), 25-27.

Fiedler, F. E. (1964). A contingency model of leadership effectiveness. In L. Berkowitz (Ed.). *Advances in experimental social psychology* (Vol. 1, pp.149-190). New York, NY: Academic Press.

Fields, D. L. (2002). *Taking the measure of work: A guide to validated scales for organizational research and diagnosis.* Thousand Oaks, CA: Sage.

Fisher, C. D., & Gitelson, R. (1983). A meta-analysis of the correlates of role conflict and ambiguity. *Journal of Applied Psychology, 68*(2), 320-333.

Fischoff, B. (1991). Value elicitation: Is there anything in there? *American Psychologist, 46*(8), 835-847.

Flamholtz, E. G., & Randle, Y. (2007). *Growing pains: Transitioning from an entrepreneurship to a professionally managed firm* (4th ed.). San Francisco, CA: Jossey-Bass.

Fonne, V. M., & Mhyre, G. (1996). The effect of occupational cultures on coordination of emergency medical service aircrew. *Aviation, Space, and Environmental Medicine, 67*(6), 525-529.

Galbreath, R. (2002). *Employee turnover hurts small and large company profitability.* Retrieved from http://www.shrm.org/Research/Articles/Articles/Pages/CMS_000117.aspx

Gartner, W. B.(1985a). A conceptual framework for describing the phenomenon of new venture creation. *Academy of Management Review, 10*(4), 696-706.

Gartner, W. B. (1985b). Review of innovation and entrepreneurship. *Academy of Management Review, 12*(1), 172-175.

Gartner, W. B. (1988). Who is an "entrepreneur?" is the wrong question. *Entrepreneurship, Theory & Practice, 13*(4), 47-68.

Gartner, W. B. (1989). Some suggestions for research on entrepreneurial traits and characteristics. *Entrepreneurship, Theory &Practice, 14*(1), 27-37.

Gartner, W. B., & Bhat, S. (2000). Environmental and ownership characteristics of small businesses and their impact on development. *Journal of Small Business Management, 38*(3), 19-33.

Gatewood, R. D., & Field, H. S. (1987). A personnel selection program for small business. *Journal of Small Business, 25*(4), 16-24.

George, J. M., & Jones, G. R. (1996). The experience of work and turnover intentions: Interactive effects of value attainment, job satisfaction, and positive mood. *Journal of Applied Psychology, 81*(3), 318-325.

Gibbins, K., & Walker, I. (1993). Multiple interpretations of the Rokeach value survey. *Journal of Social Psychology, 133*(6), 797-805.

Gibbons, C. (2006). *Economic gardening*. City of Littleton Colorado Business/Industry Affairs website, p. 1-13. Retrieved from http://www.littletongov.org/bia/economicgardening/default.asp

Gibbons, C. (2010). *Economic gardening: An entrepreneurial approach to economic development*. City of Littleton, CO. Retrieved from http://www.littletongov.org/fia/economicgardening/default/asp

Gibbons, C., & Lange, M. (2010). *Economic gardening: Past, present, and future*. 8th Annual International Economic Gardening Conference: Center for Economic Vitality, Western Washington University at Bellingham, WA.

Gilbert, G. R. (1985). Building highly productive work teams through positive leadership. *Public Personnel Management, 14*(4), 449-454.

Graen, G. B., & Cashman, J. (1975). A role-making model of leadership in formal organizations: A developmental approach. In J.G. Hunt & L. L. Lardons (Eds.), *Leadership Frontiers* (pp.143-166). Kent, OH: Kent State University Press.

Graen, G. B., & Uhl-Bien, M. (1991). The transformation of professionals into self-managing and partially self-designing contributors: Toward a theory of leadership-making. *Journal of Management Systems, 3*(3), 25-39.

Graen, G. B., & Uhl-Bien, M. (1995). Relationship-based approaches to leadership: Development of leader member exchange (LMX) theory of leadership over 25 years. Applying a multi-level, multi-domain perspective. *Leadership Quarterly, 6*(2), 219-247.

Graen, G., Dansereau, F., Minami, T., & Cashman, J. (1973). Leadership behaviors as cues to performance evaluation. *Academy of Management Journal, 16*(4), 611-623.

Greenleaf, R. (1977). *Servant leadership: A journey into the nature of legitimate power and greatness* (25th anniversary ed.). Mahwah, NJ: Paulist Press.

Griffin, R. W., & Moorhead, G. (2010). *Organizational behavior: Managing people & organizations* (9th ed.). New York, NY: South-Western Cengage Learning.

Gundry, L. K., & Welsch, H. P. (2001). The ambitious entrepreneur: High growth strategies of women-owned enterprises. *Journal of Business Venturing, 16*(5), 453-470.

Hackman, M. Z., & Johnson, C. E. (2009). *Leadership, a communication perspective* (5th ed.). Long Grove, IL: Waveland Press.

Harris, J. H., & Arendt, L. A. (1988). Stress reduction and the small business: Increasing employee and customer satisfaction. *SAM® Advanced Management Journal, 63*(1), 27- 35.

Harris, S. G., & Mossholder, K. W. (1996). The affective implications of perceived congruence with culture dimensions during organizational transformation. *Journal of Management, 22*(4), 527-547.

Haslam, S. A., & Platow, M. J. (2001). The link between leadership and followership: How affirming social identity translates into action. *Personality and Social Psychology Bulletin, 27*(11), 1469-1479. doi:10.1177/01461672012711008.

Haugh, H., & McKee, L. (2004). The cultural paradigm of the smaller firm. *Journal of Small Business Management, 42*(4), 377-394.

Heneman, H, G., III, & Berkley, R. A. (1999). Applicant attraction practices and outcomes among small business. *Journal of Small Business Management, 37*(1), 53-74.

Heneman, R. L., Tansy, J. W., & Camp, S. M. (2000). Human resource management practices in small and medium-sized enterprises: Unanswered questions and future research perspectives. *Entrepreneurship Theory and Practice, 25*(1), 11-26.

Hersey, P., & Blanchard, K. H. (1969). Life-cycle theory of leadership. *Training and Development Journal, 23*(2), 26-34.

Hisrich, R. D., Peters, M. P., & Shepherd, D. A. (2008). *Entrepreneurship* (7th ed.). New York, NY: McGraw-Hill Irwin.

Hollander, E. P. (1985). Leadership and power. In G. Lindzey &E. Aronson (Eds.), *The handbook of social psychology* (3rd ed., pp. 485-537). New York: Random House.

Hollander, E. P. (1995). Organizational leadership and followership. In P. Collett&A. Furnham (Eds.), *Social psychology at work: Essays in honor of Michael Argyle* (pp. 69-87). London: Routledge.

Homer, P., & Kahles, L. (1988). A structural equation test of the 'Value-Attitude-B-behavior Hierarchy'. *Journal of Personality and Social Psychology, 54*, 638-664.

Hornsby, J. S., & Kuratko, D. K. (1990). Human resource management in small firms: Critical issues for the 1990s. *Journal of Small Business Management, 28*(3), 9-18.

Hornsby, J. S., & Kuratko, D. F. (2003). Human resources management in small businesses: A replication and extension. *Journal of Developmental Entrepreneurship, 8*(1), 73-92.

House, R. J., Spangler, W. D., & Woycke, J. (1991). Personality and charisma in the U.S. presidency: A psychological theory of leadership effectiveness. *Administrative Science Quarterly, 36*(3), 364-396.

InfoUSA. (2011). Retrievedfromhttp://www.referenceusagov.com

International Economic Development Council [IEDC]. (2010). Five year strategic plan: 2008–2013. Retrieved from http://www.iedconline.org/

Inu, T. S. (1996). The virtue of qualitative and quantitative research. *Annals of Internal Medicine, 125*(9), 770-771.

Jehn, K., Chadwick, C., & Thatcher, S. M. (1997). To agree or not to agree: The effect of value congruence, individual demographic dissimilarity, and conflict on workgroup outcomes. *International Journal of Conflict Management, 8*(4), 287-306.

Johnson, J. E. (2003). A study of the relationship between followership modalities and leadership styles among educators at selected high schools in Jackson, Mississippi. (Unpublished doctoral dissertation). Andrews University, Berrien Springs, Michigan.

Johnston, C. S. (1995). The Rokeach value survey: Underlying structure and multidimensional scaling. *Journal of Psychology, 129*(5), 583-597.

Judge, T. A., & Bretz, D. R., Jr. (1992). Effects of work values on job choice decisions. *Journal of Applied Psychology, 77*(3), 261-271.

Judge, T. A., & Martocchio, J.J. (1992). The effect of work values on absence disciplinary decisions: The role of fairness orientation and supervisor attributions. *Center for Advanced Human Resources Studies - CHARS Working Paper Series.* Cornell University. Retrieved from http://digitalcommons.ilr.cornell.edu/cahrswp/317

Kalliath, T. J., Bluedorn, A. C., & Strube, M. J. (1999). A test of value congruence effects. *Journal of Organizational Behavior, 20*(7), 1175-1198.

Kamakura, W. A., & Mazzon, J. A. (1991). Value segmentation: A model for the measurement of values and value systems. *Journal of Consumer Research, 18*(2), 208-218.

Katz, D., & Kahn, R. L. (1978). *The social psychology of organizations* (2nd ed.). New York, NY: John Wiley & Sons.

Katz, J., & Gartner, W. B. (1988). Properties of emerging organizations. *Academy of Management Review, 13*(3), 429-441.

Kaufman Foundation & International Economic Development Council [IEDC]. (2008). *Entrepreneurship summit: Executive summary.* Kansas City, MO: Ewing Marion Kauffman Foundation.

Kelley, R. E. (1988). In praise of followers. *Harvard Business Review, 66*(6), 142-149.

Kelley, R. E. (1992). *The power of followership.* New York, NY: Doubleday.

Kotey, B., & Meredith, G. G. (1997). Relationships among owner/manager personal values, business strategies and enterprise performance. *Journal of Small Business Management, 35*(2), 37-64.

Kotey, B., & Slade, P. (2005). Formal human resource management practices in small growing firms. *Journal of Small Business Management, 43*(1), 16-41.

Kotter, J. P. (1997). Leading by vision and strategy. *Executive Excellence, 14*(10), 15-16.

Kotter, J. P. (2000). Leadership engine. *Executive Excellence, 17*(4), 7-8.

Kotter, J. P. (2006). Transformation producing change is about leadership. *Leadership Excellence, 23*(1), 14-14.

Kristoff, A. L. (1996). Person-organization fit: An integrative review of its conceptualizations, measurement and implications. *Personnel Psychology, 49*(1), 1-49.

Kunze, M. (2006). An examination of the linkages between personality, leader member exchange and experienced violation of the psychological contract. (Unpublished doctoral dissertation). Georgia State University, Atlanta.

Lee, J. (1997). Leader member exchange, the "Pelz effect," and cooperative communication between group members. *Management Communication Quarterly, 11*(2), 266-287.

Liden, R., & Maslyn, J. (1998). Multidimensionality of leader member exchange: An empirical assessment through scale development. *Journal of Management, 24*(1), 43-72.

Loewe, P., & Dominiquini, J. (2006). Overcoming effective barriers to effective innovation. *Strategy & Leadership. 34*(1), 25-31. Retrieved from the ABI/INFORM Global database. doi:10.1108/10878570610637858

Low, S., Henderson, J., & Weiler, S. (2005). Gauging a region's entrepreneurial potential. *Economic Review–Federal Reserve Bank of Kansas City, 90*(3), 61-80. Retrieved from ABI/INFORM Global. (Document ID:923905801)

Lundin, S. C., & Lancaster, L. C. (1990). Beyond leadership: The importance of followership. *The Futurist, 24*(3), *18-23.*

Maierhofer, N. I., Griffin, M. A., & Sheehan, M. (2000). Linking manager values and behavior with employee values and behavior: A study of safety in the hairdressing industry. *Journal of Occupational Health Psychology, 5*(4), 417-427.

Marlow, S., & Patton, D. (1993). Managing the employment relationship in the smaller firm: Possibilities for human resource management. *International Small Business Journal, 11*(4), 57-64.

McDonald, J. H. (2009). *Handbook of biological statistics* (2nd ed., pp. 221-223). Baltimore, MD: Sparky House. Retrieved from http://udel.edu/~mcdonald/statspearman.html.

Meglino, B. M., Ravlin, E. C., & Adkins, C. L. (1989). A work values approach to corporate culture: A field test of the value congruence process and its relationship to individual outcomes. *Journal of Applied Psychology, 74*(3), 424-432.

Meilinger, P. (1994). The ten rules of good followership. *Military Review, 74*(8), 32. Retrieved from http://www.au.af.mil/au/awc/awcgate/au-24/meilinger.pdf

Merrens, M. R., & Garret, J. B. (1975). The protestant ethic scale as a predictor of repetitive work performance. *Journal of Applied Psychology, 60*(1), 125-127. (Unpublished doctoral dissertation). Louisiana State University and Agricultural & Mechanical College, Baton Rouge.

Miethe, T. D. (1985). The validity and reliability of value measurements. *Journal of Psychology, 119*(5), 441-453.

Minsky, B. (2002). LMX dyad agreement: Construct definition and the role of supervisor/subordinate similarity and communication in understanding LMX. (Unpublished doctoral dissertation). Louisiana State University and Agricultural & Mechanical College, Baton Rouge.

Mitchell, L. (2009, October 17). *Lessons from Kauffman campuses and building an entrepreneurial ecosystem based on where you are planted.* Closing presentation at the 2009 GCEC Conference at Rice University, Houston, TX.

Moore, J. E., Munzel, M., & Pfister, S. (1998). Are the keys to improving employee retention walking out your door? *Human Resource Professional, 11*(1), 14-18.

Moore, M. (1975). Rating vs. ranking in the Rokeach value survey. An Israel comparison. *Journal of Psychology, 119*(5), 441-453.

Moorman, R. H., & Blakely, G. L. (1995). Individualism-collectivism as an individual difference predictor of organizational citizenship behavior. *Journal of Organizational Behavior, 16*(2), 127-142.

Mueller, D., & Wornhoff, S. (1990). Distinguishing personal and social values. *Educational & Psychological Measurement, 50*(3), 691-700.

Munson, J. M., & McIntyre, S. H. (1979, February). Developing practical procedures for the measurement of personal values in cross-culture marketing. *Journal of Marketing Research, 16*(1), 48-52.

Northouse, P. G. (2004). *Leadership: Theory and practice* (3rd. ed.). Thousand Oaks, CA: Sage.

Norton, M. I., Vandello, J. A., & Darley, J. M. (2004). Casuistry and social category bias. *Journal of Personality and Social Psychology, 87*(6), 817-831.

Nuseibeh, B., & Easterbrook, S. (2000). Requirements engineering: A roadmap. ICSE—future of SE track. Retrieved from http://www.doc.ic.ac.uk/~ban/pubs/sotar.re.pdf

O'Reilly, C. A., & Chatman, J. (1986). Organizational commitment and psychological attachment: The effects of compliance, identification, and internalization on prosocial behavior. *Journal of Applied Psychology, 71*(3), 492-499.

O'Reilly, C. A., Chatman, J., & Caldwell, D. F. (1991). People and organizational culture: A profile comparison approach to assessing person organization fit. *Academy of Management Journal, 34*(3), 487-516.

Overton, L. F. (1997). *The values of college and university chief financial officers as measured by the Rokeach values survey.* (Doctoral dissertation). Saint Louis University, St. Louis, MO. (OCLC No. 667207326).

Owen, H. (2000). *In search of leaders.* New York, NY: John Wiley &Sons.

Paul, J., Costley, D. L., Howell, J. P., & Dorfman, P. W. (2002). The mutability of charisma in leadership research. *Management Decision, 40*(2), 192-200.

Payne, S. L. (1988). Values and ethics-related measures for management education. *Journal of Business Ethics, 7*(4), 273-277. Retrieved from http://www.getcited.org/pub/103351462

Pearce, C. L., Maciariello, J. A., & Yamawaki, H. (2010). *The Drucker difference: What the world's greatest management thinker means to today's business leaders.* New York, NY: McGraw Hill.

Philbrick, J. H., Dart, B. D., & Hass, M. E. (1999). Pre-employment screening: A decade of change. *American Business Review, 17*(2), 75-86.

Phillips, A., & Bedeian, A. (1994). Leader-follower exchange quality: The role of personal and interpersonal attributes. *Academy of Management Journal, 37*(4), 990-1001.

Pillis, E. D., & Reardon, K. K. (2007). The influence of personality traits and persuasive messages on entrepreneurial intention: a cross cultural comparison. *Career Development International, 12*(4), 382-396. doi:10:1108/136204307/10756762

Pitts, R. E., & Woodside, A. G. (1983, February). Personal value influences on consumer product class and brand preferences. *Journal of Social Psychology, 119*(1), 37-53.

Posner, B. Z. (1992). Person-organization values congruence: No support for individual differences as a moderating influence. *Human Relations, 45*(4), 351-361.

Posner, B. Z. (2010). Values and the American manager: A three-decade perspective. *Journal of Business Ethics, 91*(4), 457-465. Retrieved from http://philpapers.org/rec/POSVAT

Posner, B. Z., Kouzes, J. M., & Schmidt, W. H. (1985). Shared values make a difference. An empirical test of corporate culture. *Human Resource Management, 24*(3), 293-309.

Posner, B. Z., & Schmidt, W. H. (1992). Values and the American manager: An update updated. *California Management Review, 34*(3), 622-648.

Purcell, J. (1993). The challenge of human resource management for industrial relations research and practice. *International Journal of Human Resource Management, 4*(3), 511-527.

Quello, S. (2010). *Program models: Part b–GrowFL™ model*. 8th Annual International Economic Gardening Conference. Center for Economic Vitality, Western Washington University: Bellingham, WA

Raosoft®. (2011). Sample size calculator by Raosoft®. Retrieved from http://www.raosoft.com/samplesize.html

Rankin, W. L., & Grube, J. W. (1980). A comparison of ranking and rating procedures for value systems measurement. *European Journal of Psychology, 10*(3), 233-246.

Rauch, C. F., & Behling, O. (1984). Functionalism: Basis for an alternate approach to the study of leadership. In J.G. Hunt, D.M. Hosking, C.A. Schriesheim, & R. Stewarts (Eds.), *Leaders and managers: International perspectives on managerial behavior and leadership,*(pp.45-62). Elmsford, NY: Pergamon Press.

Ravlin, E. C., & Meglino, B. M. (1987). The effect of values in perceptions and decision-making: A study of alternative work values measures. *Journal of Applied Psychology, 72*(4), 666- 673.

Ray, J. J. (1970). The development and validation of a balance dogmatism scale. *Australian Journal of Psychology, 22*(3), 253-260. Retrieved from http://jonjayray.tripod.com/baldog1.html

Reswick, J. (1994). What constitutes valid research? Qualitative vs. quantitative research. *Journal of Rehabilitation Research & Development, 31*(2), 7-10.

Richards, D., & Engle, S. (1986). After the vision: Suggestions to corporate visionaries and vision champions. In J.D. Adams (Ed.), *Transforming leadership* (p.199-214).Alexandria, VA: Miles River Press.

Robinson, G. (1999, January-February). Leadership vs. management. *The British Journal of Administrative Management,* 20-21.

Rogoff, E., Lee, M., & Suh, D. (2004). Who done it? Attributions by entrepreneurs and experts of the factors that cause and impede small business success. *Journal of Small Business Management, 42*(4), 364-377.

Rokeach, M. (1968). *Beliefs, attitudes, and values: A theory of organization and change.* San Francisco, CA: Jossey-Bass.

Rokeach, M. (1973). *The nature of human values.* New York, NY: Free Press.

Rokeach, M., & Ball-Rokeach, S. J. (1989). Stability and change in American value priorities, 1968-1981. *American Psychologist, 44*(5), 775-784.

Rosenau, J. (2004). Followership and discretion: Assessing the dynamics of modern leadership. *Harvard International Review, 26*(3), 14-18.

Rowden, R. (2002). The relationship between workplace learning and job satisfaction in U.S. small to midsize businesses. *Human Resources Development Quarterly, 13*(4), 407-425.

Rural Policy Research Institute [RUPRI].(2008). *Riverlands economic advantage partnership charting a new economic future.* RUPRI Center for Regional Competiveness: University of Missouri-Columbia. Retrieved from http://www.rupri.org

Rural Policy Research Institute [RUPRI]. (2009, Spring). *Strategic economic opportunities for the Riverlands: Reaching for new horizons.* RUPRI Center for Regional Competiveness: University of Missouri-Columbia.

Rusher, M. (2005). A case study of followership in the charter schools of Washtenaw County, Michigan. (Unpublished doctoral dissertation).Capella University, Minneapolis, MN.

Saks, A. M., & Ashforth, B. E. (1997). A longitudinal investigation of relationships between job information sources, applicant perceptions or fit, and work outcomes. *Personnel Psychology, 50*(2), 395-426.

Scandura, T. A. (1999). Rethinking leader member exchange: An organizational justice perspective. *Leadership Quarterly, 10*(1), 25-41.

Schein, E. H. (1985). *Organizational culture and leadership.* San Francisco, CA: Jossey-Bass.

Schneider, B. (1987). The people make the place. *Personnel Psychology, 40*(3), 437-453.

Schwartz, S. H., & Bilsky, W. (1987). Toward a universal psychological structure of human values. *Journal of Personality and Social Psychology*, *53*(3), 550-562.

Scott, R. (2003). *Organizations: Rational, natural, and open systems.* Upper Saddle River, NJ: Pearson Education.

Sergiovanni, T. J. (1990). Adding value to leadership gets extraordinary results. *Educational Leadership*, *47*(8), 23-27.

Sharma, A. S. (1997). Leadership: The manager vs. the leader. Occasional Paper No. 5, New Zealand Teacher's Council, *29*(9),*34-35.*New South Wales, Department of Education, New Zealand.

Sherwood, D. (2002). *Innovation express.* New York, NY: Capstone.

Simon, M. & Francis, B. (2001*). The dissertation and research cookbook*, 3rd Ed. Dubuque, IA: Kendall- Hunt.

Skinner, B. F. (1971). *Beyond freedom and dignity.* New York, NY: Knopf.

Small Business Administration. (2006). Retrieved from Small Business Administration website: http://www.sba.gov.

Smith, A. (2003). *The wealth of nations* (Reprinted). New York, NY: Bantam Classics (Original work published in 1776).

Sobel, R. S.(2006, August 28). Entrepreneurship. *The concise encyclopedia of economics.* Retrieved from http://www.be.wvu.edu/divecon/econ/sobel/Entr/

Solovy, A. (2005). Followership. *Hospitals and Health Networks, 78*(5), 32-33. Retrieved from http://www.biomedexperts.com/Profile.bme/1330612/Alden_Solovy

Southwestern Wisconsin Regional Planning Commission [SWRPC]. (2009, June). *2009- 2014 comprehensive economic development strategy: 2009-2010 annual report.* Southwestern Wisconsin Economic Development District. Retrieved from http://www.swwrpc.org/

Spangenburg, J. (2004). An empirical evaluation of the effects of federal downsizing on select organizational variables.(Unpublished doctoral dissertation). Regent University, Virginia Beach, VA.

Sparrowe, R., & Liden, R. (1997). Process and structure in leader member exchange. *The Academy of Management Review, 22*(2), 522-535.

Stavrou, E., Kleanthous, T., & Anastasiou, T. (2005). Leadership personality and firm culture during hereditary transitions in family firms: Model development and empirical investigation. *Journal of Small Business Management, 43*(2), 187-207.

Steinback, T. (2010, June). *Riverlands stage 2 survey executive summary.* Platteville, WI: University of Wisconsin Platteville.

Stewart, T. (2003). Digging deeply, seeing widely. *Harvard Business Review, 81*(4), 10.

Storey, D. J. (1994). *Understanding the small business sector.* London: Routledge.

Survey Monkey (2012). Retrieved from www.surveymonkey.com.

Tabachnick, B. G., & Fidell, L. S. (2007). Using multivariate statistics (5th ed.). Boston, MA: Pearson Education.

Tetlock, P. E. (1986, April). A value pluralism model of ideological reasoning. *Journal of Personality and Social Psychology, 50,* 819-827.

Toler, C. (1975, July). The personal values of alcoholics and addicts. *Journal of Clinical Psychology, 31*(3), 554-557.

U.S. Department of Commerce, Economic Development Administration [EDA]. (2010a). *EDA 2010 investment policies.* Retrieved from http://www.eda.gov/PDF/EDA %20Collateral%20Piece_With%202010%20Investment%20Policies.pdf

U.S. Department of Commerce, Economic Development Administration [EDA]. (2010b). *EDA a key Federal player in unlocking regional and local economic development.* Retrieved from http://www.nado.org/conference_files/taylor.pdf

U.S. Department of Commerce, Economic Development Administration [EDA]. (2010c). *EDA overview of grant process.* Retrieved from http://www.eda.gov/.../061809 %20EDA%20Grant%20Process%20FINAL.ppt

Wiklund, J., Davidson, P., & Delmar, F. (2003, Spring). What do they think and feel about growth? An expectancy-value approach to small business managers' attitudes toward growth. *Entrepreneurship: Theory & Practice, 27*(3), 247-270.

Wilhelm, C., Herd, A., & Steiner, D. (1993). Attributional conflict between managers and subordinates: An investigation of leader member exchange effects. *Journal of Organizational Behavior, 14*(6), 531-544.

Williams, P. M. (2001). Building an ecological model of employee retention in very small businesses. (Unpublished doctoral dissertation). Graduate School of Saint Louis University, St. Louis, MO.

Williams, R. M., Jr. (1979). Change and stability in values and value systems: A sociological perspective. In M. Rokeach (Ed.), *Understanding human values, individual and societal.* (p. 15-46). New York, NY: Free Press.

Wood, J. (2010). *The Wisconsin way: Blueprint for change 2010.* Retrieved fromhttp:www.wisconsinway.org/BluePrintForChange.pdf

Wren, J. T. (1995). *The leader's companion: Insights on leadership through the ages.* New York, NY: The Free Press.

Yukl, G. A. (2002). *Leadership in organizations* (2nd ed.). Upper Saddle River, NJ: Prentice Hall.

Zakaria, F. (2009). *The post-American world.* New York, NY: Norton.

Zaleznik, A. (1992). Managers and leaders: Are they different? *Harvard Business Review, 70*(2), 126-136.

APPENDICES

APPENDIX A: The Leader-Member Exchange (LMX) Model

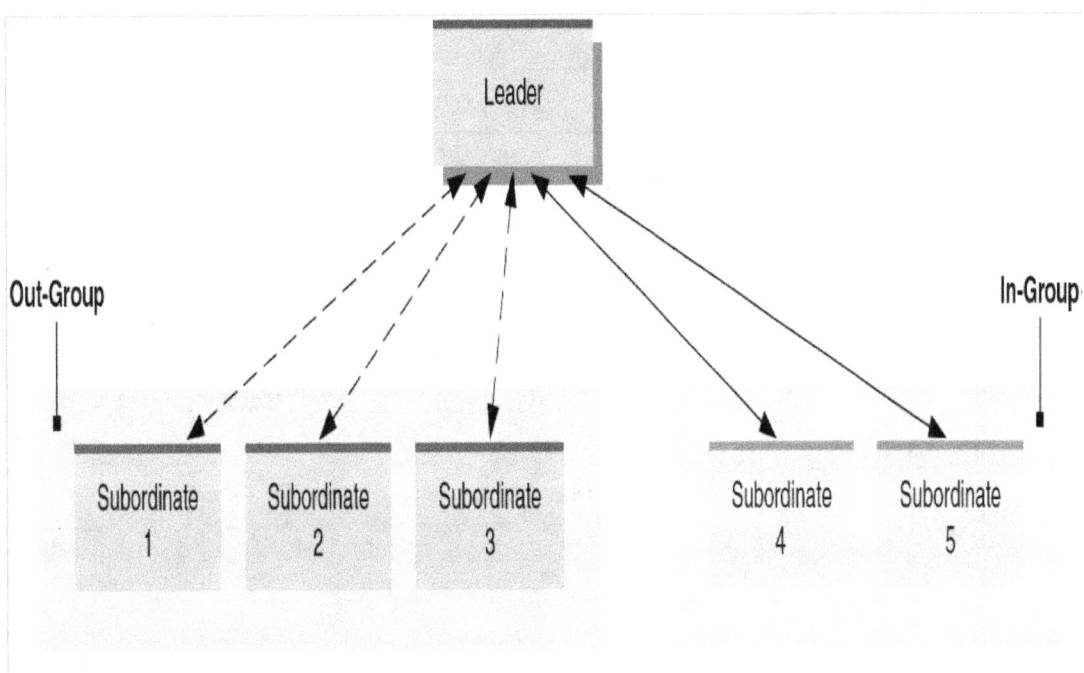

Figure A1. The LMX model suggests that leaders form unique independent relationshipswith each of their subordinates. As illustrated here, a key factor in the nature of this relationship is whether the individual subordinate is in the leader's out-group or in-group. Adapted from "Organizational Behavior: Managing People & Organizations," (9th ed.) by R. W. Griffin and G. Moorhead, 2010, p. 333. Copyright 2010 by South-Western Cengage Learning.

APPENDIX B: Stage 2 Business Clusters Across Dubuque Tri-States Market

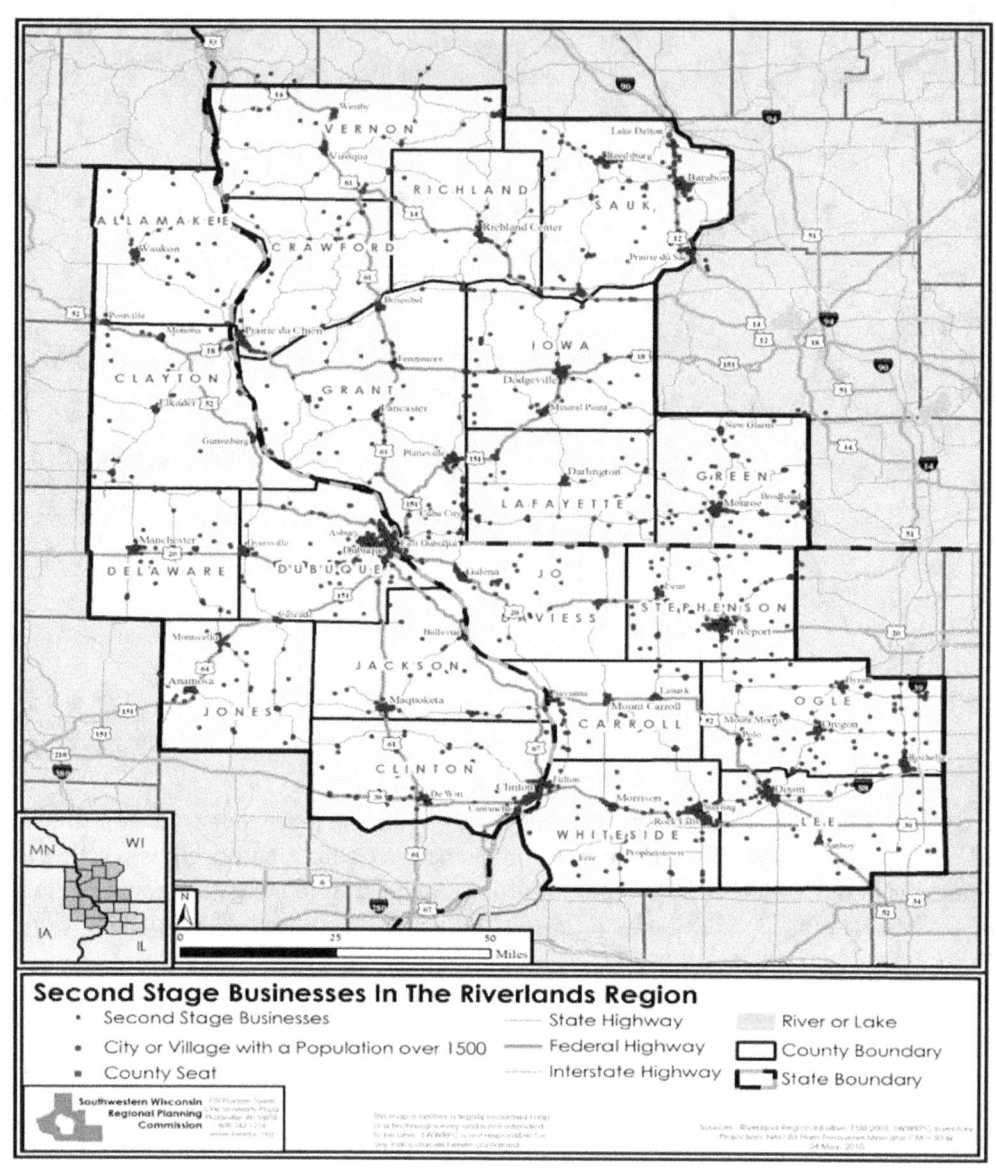

Note: Adapted from 2009-2014 Comprehensive Economic Development Strategy: 2009-2010 Annual Report, by Southwest Wisconsin Regional Planning Commission, 2009. Copyright 2009 by the Southwestern Wisconsin Regional Planning Commission.

APPENDIX C: Tri-States LMX Survey 2012

Tri-States LMX Survey 2012
Thomas R. Steinback, Principle Investigator
Argosy University Online
yankeefaninia@yahoo.com   563-581-3720

WELCOME TO THE TRI-STATES LMX SURVEY 2012!   Date

Your Company was cordially invited to participate in this research study focusing on the unique relationship between small business leaders (managers) and their followers (employees). Specifically, what are the values and associated behaviors a leader deems as most and least important for their followers to demonstrate for the business to achieve and sustain success? Further, we want to examine those values and associated behaviors the leader deems most and least important to their personal success as a leader. Each company owner/site manager or their leader designee, represent one of 278 randomly selected private businesses that employee 10-499 employees across the Tri-States.

My name is Tom Steinback and I am a doctoral candidate at Argosy University. This is a degree requirement and major component to my DBA dissertation research effort and your assistance is appreciated. A hard copy of the online survey has been provided for your convenience. Page 1 explains the elements of informed consent as it pertains to internet surveys, page 2 is Demographics, page 3 is Scenario One, page 4 is Scenario Two, and page 5 is where participants may choose to submit the survey. Every page has an 'Exit This Survey' button on the top right hand corner of the page. Your participation will take approximately 10-15 minutes to complete the survey and your participation in this research is strictly voluntary. You may refuse to participate at all or at any point in the research, without fear of penalty of negative consequence of any kind.

The information you provide for this research will be treated confidentially and all raw data will be kept in a secured file by the principle investigator. Results of the research will be reported as aggregate summary data only, and no individually identifiable information will be presented. You also have the right to review the results of the research if you wish to do so. A copy of the summary report will automatically be emailed to all invitees for whom an email address was identified and validated, whether they participated or not. There will be no direct or immediate personal benefits from your participation in this research.
If you choose to voluntarily participate, simply use the confidential survey web-link on the back of my business card: https:www.research.net/s/25HGYZY, and password, tristates2012. Once participants arrive at the survey website, they should carefully read the elements of informed consent on page one. On question one in the Demographics section, participants are required to enter a unique 4 digit code, such as 9999. The web-link, password and unique 4 digit code are on the back of my business card. Finally, at the end of the survey, participants may choose to hit the "Submit" button. For your information and convenience, a hard copy of this cover letter, my business card, and a hard copy of the online survey is enclosed with this packet. DO NOT Return any material to us. It is copy-righted and may not be reproduced or distributed without permission.

If you would like to receive an emailed copy of the final survey summary report, please be sure to send your email address to me at the email address at the top of this letter. Thank you for your time and interest,

Tom Steinback

Elements of Informed Consent (Alternative Consent Form)
Page 1 of 5

You are cordially invited to participate in a research study. The purpose of this research study is to study the unique relationship between small business leaders (managers) and their followers (employees) -- Specifically, what are the values and associated behaviors a leader deems as most important and least important for followers to demonstrate for your business to achieve success, and for their personal success as a leader. This research study is a degree requirement of Tom Steinback's DBA dissertation program. You are being asked to participate because you are the owner/site manager or leader designee, of a small business in the Tri-States. If you participate in this research, you will be asked to complete three tasks: Part 1 consists of 8 demographic questions; Part 2 Scenario One and asks you to rank order an alphabetical list of 18 items; Part 3 Scenario Two asks you to rank order the same list of items. Your participation will take approximately 10-15 minutes.

Your participation in this research is strictly voluntary. You may refuse to participate at all, or choose to stop your participation at any point in the research, without fear of penalty or negative consequences of any kind. The information/data you provide for this research will be treated confidentially, and all raw data will be kept in a secured file by the principal investigator. Results of the research will be reported as aggregate summary data only, and no individually identifiable information will be presented.

You also have the right to review the results of the research if you wish to do so. A copy of the results may be obtained by contacting the principal investigator as follows: Tom Steinback , Principle Investigator, yankeefaninia@yahoo.com, 563-581-3720.

There will be no direct or immediate personal benefits from your participation in this research.

Informed Consent means you affirm: You understand that this research study has been reviewed and Certified by the Argosy University Online Institutional Review Board. For research-related problems or questions regarding participant rights, you can contact Dr. Nancy Hoover, AUO IRB Contact, (nhoover@argosy.edu). You have read and understand the information explaining the purpose of this research and your rights and responsibilities as a participant. Since this is an anonymous internet based survey, your consent in lieu of a signature will be signified by entering the unique 4 digit code given to you in question one on page 2 and by hitting the submit button on page 5.

Thank you for participating!

PART ONE -- DEMOGRAPHIC INFORMATION:
Page 2 of 5

BEFORE WE BEGIN, Survey participants are respectfully requested to answer the 8 demographic questions below as each applies to them. No Personal Identifying information is requested.

1. **Survey Code:** Enter the four digit numeric code as provided with the survey login instructions this question is mandatory: _ _ _ _

2. **Location:** Which Tri-States County is your business located in?
    O DUBUQUE, IA O GRANT, WI O JO DAVIESS, IL   O Rather Not Say

3. **NAICS Industry:** Check box for the Industry in which your business competes
    (for example: manufacturing, OR retailing, OR public accounting).
    O Agriculture, Forestry, Fishing & Hunting   O Mining, Quarrying, Oil & Gas Extraction
    O Utilities   O Construction
    O Manufacturing   O Wholesale Trade
    O Retail Trade   O Transportation & Warehousing
    O Information   O Finance & Insurance
    O Real Estate, Rental & Leasing   O Professional, Scientific, Technical Services
    O Management of Companies & Enterprises   O Administrative, Support, Waste Management
    O Educational Services   O Health Care & Social Assistance
    O Arts, Entertainment, Recreation   O Accommodations & Food Services
    O Other Services (NOT Public Administration)   O Public Administration

4. **Education Information** (Select the highest education level attained)
    O No High School Degree and no college   O Possess High School Degree
    O Possess Bachelor's Degree   O Possess Master's Degree
    O Possess Doctorate Degree   O Rather Not Say

5. **Total Years in Small Business Leadership Position** (Select the option that applies) O Less than 1 year O 1 to 5 years   O 6 to 10 years
    O 11 to 15 years   O 16 years or more   O Rather Not Say

6. **Age Information** (Check the option that applies)
    O 65 +   O 45 – 49   O 25 - 29
    O 60 – 64   O 40 – 44   O 20 - 24
    O 55 – 59   O 35 – 39   O 18 - 19
    O 50 – 54   O 30 – 34   O Rather Not Say

7. **Gender Information** (Check one)
    O Female   O male   O Rather Not Say

8. **Ethnic Information** (Check one)
    O African American O American Native O Caucasian
    O Hispanic   O Other   O Rather Not Say

PART TWO – SCENARIO ONE
Page 3 of 5

Question One

"What are the values and associated behaviors you as a small business leader, deem most desirable for a follower in your company (i.e., subordinates, direct reports, members, etc.) to possess and demonstrate in order for your company to achieve and sustain success?"

This is Scenario One. Imagine the ideal employee-follower in your company. This person may be someone you presently know or have known in the past. As you think of them, what values or associated behaviors did they demonstrate that made you feel they are the kind of person you want in your company? If you could 'clone' the ideal employee-follower, what values would they possess?

To begin, look at the alphabetical list of 18 instrumental values and associated behaviors below and select the value that is of most importance to you. Your goal is to rank order each value in its order of importance to you. Write the number 1 in the blank space next to that value that is most important. Next, choose the value that is second in importance to you and write the number 2 in the blank next to it. Work your way through the list until you have ranked all 18 values on this page. The value that is of least importance to you should have the number 18 in the box.

When ranking, take your time and think carefully. Feel free to go back and change your order should you have second thoughts about any of your answers. When you have completed your ranking, the result should represent an accurate picture of those values you deem most important to least important, for your employee-followers to possess. There is no right or wrong answer. Your choices are unique to you and your company setting. NO two values can share the same ranking. When you have finished ranking all 18 values, go to scenario 2 on the next page and follow instructions accordingly. Please do each page separately.

Value (Associated Behaviors) Importance Rank (1 = Most: 18 = Least)

Ambitious (hard-working, aspiring	
Broadminded (open-minded)	
Capable (competent, effective)	
Cheerful (lighthearted, joyful)	
Clean (neat, tidy)	
Courageous (standing up for your beliefs)	
Forgiving (willing to pardon others)	
Helpful (working for the welfare of others)	
Honest (sincere truthful)	
Imaginative (daring, creative)	
Independent (self-reliant, self-sufficient)	
Intellectual (intelligent, reflective)	
Logical (consistent, rational)	
Loving (affectionate, tender)	
Obedient (dutiful, respectful)	
Polite (courteous, well-mannered)	
Responsible (dependable, reliable)	
Self-controlled (restrained, self-disciplined	

PART THREE – SCENARIO TWO
Page 4 of 5

Question Two

"What are the values and behaviors you as a small business leader deem most desirable for yourself personally to possess, in order to achieve and sustain success as a leader?"

This is Scenario Two. Reflect on your personal experience as a leader in your company and imagine those values or associated behaviors that are the most important to your success as a leader. Which values and associated behaviors are the most important, and which are the least important?

To begin, look at the alphabetical list of 18 instrumental values and associated behaviors below and select the value that is of most importance to you. Your goal is to rank order each value in its order of importance to you. Write the number 1 in the blank space next to that value that is most important. Next, choose the value that is second in importance to you and write the number 2 in the blank next to it. Work your way through the list until you have ranked all 18 values on this page. The value that is of least importance to you should have the number 18 in the box.

When ranking, take your time and think carefully. Feel free to go back and change your order should you have second thoughts about any of your answers. When you have completed your ranking, the result should represent an accurate picture of those values you deem most important to least important, for successful leaders to possess. There is no right or wrong answer. Your choices are unique to you and your company setting. NO two values can share the same ranking.

When you have finished ranking all 18 values, go to the next page.
Value (Associated Behaviors) Importance Rank (1 = Most: 18 = Least)

Value (Associated Behaviors)	Rank
Ambitious (hard-working, aspiring	
Broadminded (open-minded)	
Capable (competent, effective)	
Cheerful (lighthearted, joyful)	
Clean (neat, tidy)	
Courageous (standing up for your beliefs)	
Forgiving (willing to pardon others)	
Helpful (working for the welfare of others)	
Honest (sincere truthful)	
Imaginative (daring, creative)	
Independent (self-reliant, self-sufficient)	
Intellectual (intelligent, reflective)	
Logical (consistent, rational)	
Loving (affectionate, tender)	
Obedient (dutiful, respectful)	
Polite (courteous, well-mannered)	
Responsible (dependable, reliable)	
Self-controlled (restrained, self-disciplined	

Note: Part Two 2 & 3 adapted from: Creative Commons Corporation, 2011, and Deckert, 2007.

THANK YOU!
Page 5 of 5

I have read the cover letter detailing the purpose and procedures for this research and I am completing this survey as evidence of my consent to be a participant in this research project. My active consent in lieu of a signature is signified by hitting the SUBMIT button below.

APPENDIX D: Five Big Ideas Behind Complexity Economics

Five Big Ideas that Distinguish Complexity Economics from Traditional Economics		
	Complexity Economics	**Traditional Economics**
Dynamics	Open, dynamic, nonlinear systems, far from equilibrium	Closed, static, linear systems in equilibrium
Agents	Modeled individually; uses inductive rules of thumb to make decisions; has incomplete information; is subject to errors and biases; learns and adapts over time	Modeled collectively; uses complex deductive calculations to make decisions; has complete information; makes no errors and has no biases; has no need for learning or adaptation (are already perfect)
Networks	Explicitly model interactions between agents; networks of relationships change over time	Assume agents only interact indirectly through market mechanisms (e.g., auctions)
Emergence	No distinction between micro and macroeconomics; macro patterns are emergent result of micro-level behaviors and interactions	Micro- and macroeconomics remain separate disciplines
Evolution	The evolutionary process of differentiation, selection, and amplification provides the system with novelty and is responsible for its growth in order and complexity	No mechanism for endogenously creating novelty, or growth in order and complexity

Note: Adapted from *The Origin of Wealth: The Radical Remaking of Economics and What it Means for Business and Society*, by E. D. Beinhocker, 2007, p. 97. Copyright 2007 by Harvard Business School Press.

APPENDIX E: Entrepreneurship Competency Model

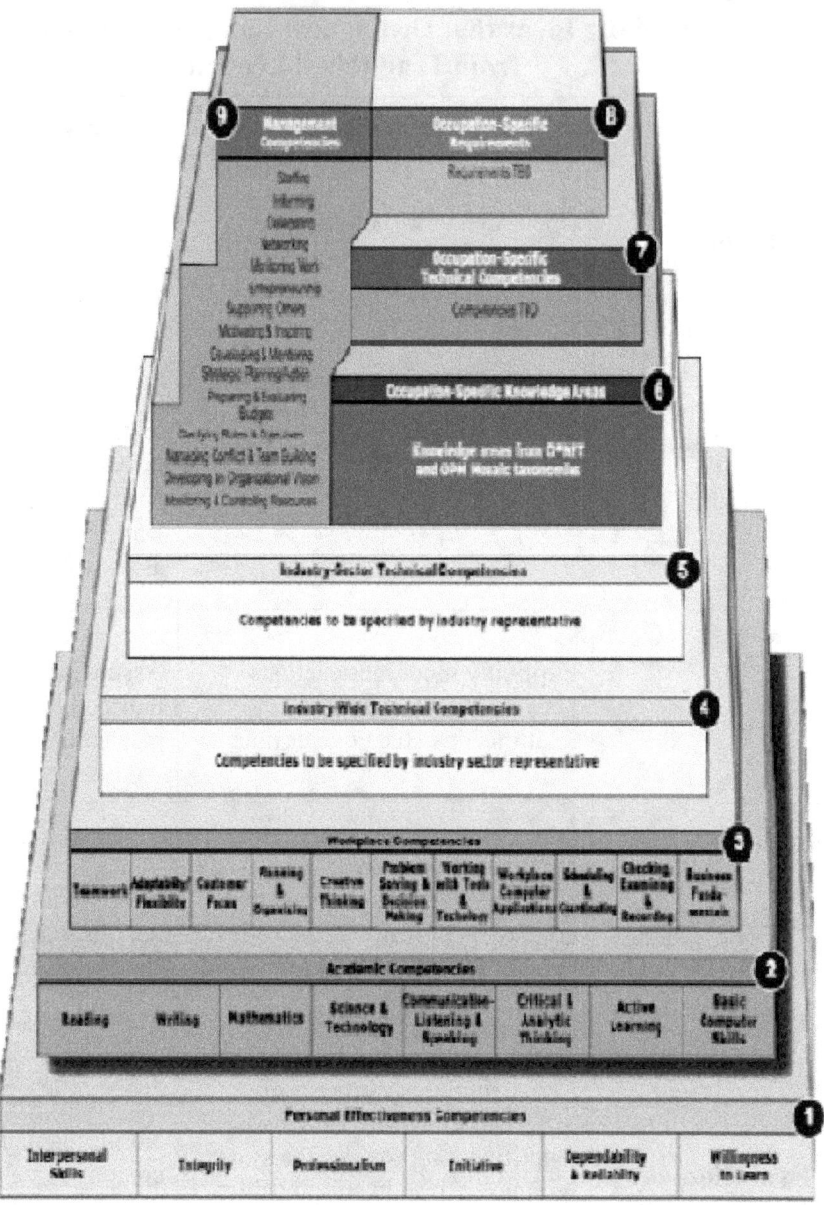

Note: Adapted from "Competency Models: A Review of the Literature and the Role of Employment and Training Administration (ETA)," by M. R. Ennis, 2009. Copyright 2008 by U. S. Department of Labor.

APPENDIX F: RVS Permissions- Attribution-ShareAlike 3.0 Unported

(CC BY-SA 3.0)

This is a human-readable summary of the Legal code (the full license). Disclaimer

You are free

- **to Share**- to copy, distribute and transmit the work
- **to Remix**- to adapt the work
- to make commercial use of the work

Under the following conditions

- **Attribution** — You must attribute the work in the manner specified by the author or licensor (but not in any way that suggests that they endorse you or your use of the work).
- **Share Alike** — If you alter, transform, or build upon this work, you may distribute the resulting work only under the same or similar license to this one.

With the understanding that

- **Waiver** — Any of the above conditions can be waived if you get permission from the copyright holder.
- **Public Domain**- Where the work or any of its elements is in the public domain under applicable law, that status is in no way affected by the license.
- **Other Rights**- In no way are any of the following rights affected by the license:
  - Your fair dealing or fair use rights, or other applicable copyright exceptions and limitations;
  - The author's moral rights;
  - Rights other persons may have either in the work itself or in how the work is used, such as publicity or privacy rights.
- **Notice**- For any reuse or distribution, you must make clear to others the license terms of this work. The best way to do this is with a link to this web page.

APPENDIX G: Demographic Data Frequency Tables

Appendix G-1: NAICS Industry
Check box for the Industry in which your business competes
(for example: manufacturing, OR retailing, OR public accounting).

		Frequency	Percent	Valid Percent	Cumulative Percent
Valid	11 Agriculture, Forestry, Fishing & Hunting	3	2.7	2.7	2.7
	23 Construction	5	4.5	4.5	7.2
	31 Manufacturing	6	5.4	5.4	12.6
	42 Wholesale Trade	4	3.6	3.6	16.2
	44 Retail Trade	24	21.4	21.6	37.8
	51 Information	1	.9	.9	38.7
	52 Finance & Insurance	7	6.3	6.3	45.0
	53 Real Estate, Rental & Leasing	5	4.5	4.5	49.5
	54 Professional, Scientific, Technical Services	9	8.0	8.1	57.7
	61 Educational Services	6	5.4	5.4	63.1
	62 Health Care & Social Assistance	12	10.7	10.8	73.9
	71 Arts, Entertainment, Recreation	4	3.6	3.6	77.5
	72 Accommodations & Food Services	13	11.6	11.7	89.2
	81 Other Services, (NOT Public Administration)	11	9.8	9.9	99.1
	92 Public Administration	1	.9	.9	100.0
	Total	111	99.1	100.0	
Missing	System	1	.9		
Total		112	100.0		

Appendix G-2: Education Information
(Please select the highest education level attained)

		Frequency	Percent	Valid Percent	Cumulative Percent
Valid	No High School Degree and No College	1	.9	.9	.9
	High School Diploma	27	24.1	24.1	25.0
	Associate's (2 year) Degree	14	12.5	12.5	37.5
	Bachelor's (4 year) Degree	45	40.2	40.2	77.7
	Master's Degree	11	9.8	9.8	87.5
	Doctorate	14	12.5	12.5	100.0
	Total	112	100.0	100.0	

Appendix G-3: Total Years in Small Business Leadership Position
(Check one)

		Frequency	Percent	Valid Percent	Cumulative Percent
Valid	Less than 1 year	12	10.7	10.7	10.7
	1 - 5 years	24	21.4	21.4	32.1
	6 - 10 years	22	19.6	19.6	51.8
	11- 15 years	16	14.3	14.3	66.1
	16 - 20 years	14	12.5	12.5	78.6
	21 years or more	24	21.4	21.4	100.0
	Total	112	100.0	100.0	

Appendix G-4: Age Information
(Check one)

		Frequency	Percent	Valid Percent	Cumulative Percent
	65+	6	5.4	5.4	5.4
	60 - 64	8	7.1	7.1	12.5
	55 - 59	13	11.6	11.6	24.1
	50 - 54	14	12.5	12.5	36.6
	45 - 49	19	17.0	17.0	53.6
Valid	40 - 44	9	8.0	8.0	61.6
	35 - 39	7	6.3	6.3	67.9
	30 - 34	8	7.1	7.1	75.0
	25 - 29	18	16.1	16.1	91.1
	20 - 24	10	8.9	8.9	100.0
	Total	112	100.0	100.0	

Appendix G-5: Gender Information
(Check one)

		Frequency	Percent	Valid Percent	Cumulative Percent
	Female	42	37.5	38.2	38.2
Valid	Male	68	60.7	61.8	100.0
	Total	110	98.2	100.0	
Missing	System	2	1.8		
Total		112	100.0		

Appendix G-6: Ethnic Information: (Check one)

		Frequency	Percent	Valid Percent	Cumulative Percent
Valid	African American	1	.9	.9	.9
	Caucasian	107	95.5	95.5	96.4
	Other	2	1.8	1.8	98.2
	Rather Not Say	2	1.8	1.8	100.0
	Total	112	100.0	100.0	

ABOUT THE AUTHOR

Dr. Thomas R. Steinback, MBA, SPHR

Dr. Steinback is a serial social entrepreneur, innovator, executive coach, and senior consulting HR business partner, helping hundreds of small business owners succeed in their quest to create wealth, survive and thrive. He is certified for life as a Senior Professional in Human Resources by the Society of Human Resource Management and serves the 2013 AZSHRM State Council as Membership Director.

Tom has over 30+ years of leadership experience in private for-profit and non-profit settings with global companies as large as GE. As an educator, he is a course creator, has served on the faculty of several higher learning institutions, instructor of adult learners in a diverse variety of undergraduate and graduate degree programs and adapted 40 courses for online learning.

He was principle investigator for several research projects examining economic gardening, small business development, leader-follower exchange, global multicultural diversity & business ethics. He is a recipient of the Governor's Certificate of Commendation in the State of Wisconsin and a Certificate of Meritorious Service from the Board of Regents of the UW System.

He earned his Bachelor of Arts in communications and religion from Ambassador University in Hertfordshire, England; his MBA in organizational development, personnel & industrial relations at Syracuse University; and his DBA in executive management from Argosy University.

His research focused on value based leadership and his Dissertation was entitled: *"Followership in the Heartland: Values and Behaviors Deemed Most Desirable by Small Business Leaders."*